Criticism in Focus

JANE AUSTEN

Graham Handley

Bristol Classical Press

For John Aston,
in warm friendship and respect

First published in 1992 by
Bristol Classical Press
an imprint of
Gerald Duckworth & Co. Ltd
48 Hoxton Square
London N1 6PB

A catalogue for this book is available
from the British Library.

ISBN 1-85399-162-7

Printed in Great Britain by
The Cromwell Press, Melksham, Wiltshire

Contents

Acknowledgements

I am grateful to Frances and Roland Hills for reading through my typescript and for their helpful comments on it. I am grateful too to Chelsey Fox for her help and guidance as always.

Graham Handley
March 1992

Introduction

In 1982 David Gilson published his bibliography of Jane Austen. As the Oxford University Press catalogue puts it, it is 'based on Sir Geoffrey Keynes' 1929 Nonesuch Press bibliography, but while retaining and expanding the original book's basic structure it is in most respects a new work'. Its 900 pages are an eloquent and factual testimony to the enduring popularity of Jane Austen, so much so that one fears that any updating in its turn, because of the volume of work to be found about her, will be too expensive to undertake. If one were to need further evidence of the minute examination of her times and her works, then this is provided in the publications of the Jane Austen Society and in the magisterial *The Jane Austen Handbook* (ed. J. David Grey, 1986). I am indebted to both on two counts: first, for introducing me to a number of areas of knowledge and comment which are not encompassed by the simple definitions of scholarship and criticism. Second, for making me, I hope, more fully responsive to the novels as sheer entertainment arising from their local context and historical time, enhancing both by their wit, their wisdom, their humanity, and furthering my delight at being caught again and again in the meshes of their narrative.

The Jane Austen Handbook contains excellent summaries of the particular periods of criticism and scholarship. This is not surprising, as they are written by Joseph Duffy, Brian Southam and Walton Litz, each of whom (and particularly the last two) has made inroads into the study of Jane Austen. But I got the impression that they were tied to limited space, unable to give more than passing evaluative commentary on people they respected and admired. In writing this short

1

guide, I have experienced the same or similar pressures and, like them, I am aware of worthy omissions. The developing depth from the bland and emollient *Biographical Notice* through to a modern explorer like Tony Tanner or a feminist critic like Margaret Kirkham is not, I think, difficult to follow. What is difficult, however, is the process of selection, and in order to give anyone studying Jane Austen the flavour of the criticism or scholarship involved, I have dwelt in some detail on each book mentioned. Also, I have deliberately chosen some books where I do not wholly agree with the views given, since I feel that part of the richness and discovery of Jane Austen lies in the way her writing yields layers of interpretation, apart from the reasonably obvious and central one. I have also included the occasional work by an acknowledged Janeite, for example, Elizabeth Jenkins, where I feel that the contribution is both positive and sympathetic. The aim of biography, criticism and scholarship should be to send the reader, whether general reader or academic student, to the text of the novels which are in the mainstream of our literary heritage. We have come a long way since F.R. Leavis' *The Great Tradition* (1948), but we should not forget his words on Jane Austen if we hope to see her whole:

> In fact, Jane Austen, in her indebtedness to others, provides an exceptionally illuminating study of the nature of originality, and she exemplifies beautifully the relations of 'the individual talent' to tradition. If the influences bearing on her hadn't comprised something fairly to be called tradition she couldn't have found herself and her true direction; but her relation to tradition is a creative one. She not only makes tradition for those coming after, but her achievement has for us a retroactive effect: as we look back beyond her we see what goes before, and see because of her, potentialities and significances brought out in such a way that, for us, she creates the tradition we see leading down to her. Her work, like the work of all great creative writers, gives a meaning to the past.

I have given this full and justifiably elevated evaluation because I feel that it embodies what most writers, who are themselves evaluated in part here, believe, that Jane Austen's greatness has only come to be fully recognized – and even now not fully defined – in our own century. This short book presents a selection of those who have written with positive discernment about the nature of that greatness, generally or in part; or of those who have made scholarly contributions, studied manuscripts, edited letters, or undertaken biographies of Jane Austen, sometimes with due emphasis on her family. For the Jane Austen enthusiast, whether student or general reader, *The Jane Austen Handbook* is strongly recommended for its information and evaluation, none of it too heavy-handed to follow (although it is, at times, esoteric). It is a book to dip into when required, since it consists of outstanding critical pieces (such as, for example, John Bayley's 'Characterisation in Jane Austen'), through to summaries of criticism and the main scholarly and biographical investigations. At the same time, it also includes the curious and the whimsical – and one feels that Jane Austen would have appreciated many of these – such as David Gilson's 'Auction Sales', and a number of peripheral articles, for example, Janet Todd's 'Servants' and Alastair Duckworth's 'Improvements'. It caters for 'Janeites and anti-Janeites', to adopt the title of Brian Southam's article, but there is a tendency (excusable nonetheless) for articles to overlap. Particularly valuable both to the general reader and the student of Jane Austen is H. Abigail Blok's 'A Dictionary of Jane Austen's Life and Works'. This is integral to the purpose of the book, a thoughtful and compact survey which reflects its author's saturation in the family and life as well as the works.

I make no apology for including in this Introduction some detailed reference to two areas of information about Jane Austen. The first of these, F.B. Pinion's *A Jane Austen Companion* (1973), is an invaluable accompaniment to Jane Austen's life and works and must be set beside *The Jane Austen Handbook* referred to previously. Its great merit is a detailed knowledge of the novels *and* the minor works, while the sequence is so direct that it can be readily useful to the student of Jane Austen and the general reader alike. There is sound historical and social detail on the background after a brief but interesting biographical summary, and then a balanced critical survey of the fiction chronologically through to *Sanditon*, with the section on *Persuasion* which can be accepted as typical. There is an account of the writing of the novel, and this is followed by some succinct critical views by Virginia Woolf and Elizabeth Bowen on the presentation of Anne Elliot. Pinion then evaluates the characterization himself; he believes, for example, that Anne is a character possessed of deep feelings but who manages to control them. In this way she obviously differs from a heroine like Marianne Dashwood. Continuing this appraisal, he feels that Anne bears a distinct similarity to Eleanor. He feels that the tone of *Persuasion* is 'autumnal', but notes that the 'spring of felicity' returns to Anne 'with her engagement to Captain Wentworth'.

Inevitably, in a handbook of this kind, much is summary, but interwoven with that summary there are acute brief evaluations – Pinion defends the elopement of Mrs Clay and Mr Elliot by asserting that 'Both are cunning contrivers' and that the suddenness of their coming together 'has that air of ingenious invention which always appealed to Jane'. At the same time he allows that if she had had time to make revisions she would perhaps have seen the bad taste which she showed in the treatment of the Musgrove parents, and also have more successfully integrated her own recollections of Lyme Regis into the narrative. But by close attention to particular details in the structure of the narrative, Pinion shows Jane Austen's sense of tension ('The double drama at the White Hart holds the reader as by a spell'). He finds the resolution at the end 'contrived with unusual skill', and this makes him feel that Jane Austen was, ironically, growing in confidence 'in her imaginative ability to explore experience more deeply than she had ever done'. After a note on *Sanditon* there is a sensible summary of the 'general characteristics' of Jane Austen's writing, with appraisals of types of humour (including burlesque), social range, and an expression of firm belief that 'it is uncritical to condemn her for not referring in her novels to events which she could only know at second hand'.

Another critical note on Jane Austen's art is to be found in the fact that her characters are revealed and exposed by what they say and their attitudes to what they have read or merely heard about. Pinion rates very highly Jane Austen's 'apprenticeship in epistolary fiction', which gave her such an insight into imagined 'thoughts and feelings of characters in a variety of situations'. There is important stress on what Pinion calls her 'psychological realism', and one statement, simple but well-considered and truthful, shows his careful concern – 'Jane Austen provides entertainment, and a serious assessment of human conduct and values'.

Another section of particular value (apart from an admirable survey of *The Letters*, which are considered later in ch. 5) is a discussion of those writers who exerted an influence on Jane Austen's own art. This includes consideration of general 18th-century characteristics, as well as specific authors: Johnson, for example, who is valued for his 'integrity, Christian piety, and reason'. Pinion rightly feels that Jane Austen sometimes employed his 'cadences', though her style is more limpid and variegated than his. The influence of 'Gilpin on the Picturesque' is admirably charted throughout her earlier works: Richardson and Fanny Burney command pride of place, but Pinion contends that the reader of Fanny Burney and then Jane Austen will recognize just how far Jane Austen's novels evince her more sophisticated and structured narrative treatment. Her novels are artistic wholes, based on realistic presentation of character seen in convincing situations and interactions, with personality in stages of development as a result. Pinion feels that these qualities are generally absent from Fanny Burney's work. Obviously Charlotte Smith and Mrs Radcliffe are important in establishing Jane Austen's own perspective on the novel, while Shakespeare, Cowper and Crabbe are more than token points of reference in her writings: Pinion points out that she uses the last Act of *The Merchant of Venice* in ch. 11 of *Mansfield Park*.

'People and Places in Jane Austen's Fiction' is a concise dictionary, and there is also a useful glossary of words where the meanings have changed since Jane Austen's time. The clarity of this modest overview of Jane Austen gives it a particular appeal derived from its obvious sympathetic affinity with its subject.

The *Collected Reports* of the Jane Austen Society (so far in 3 vols, 1949-65, 1966-75 and 1976-85) provide a valuable commentary on the increasing interest in Jane Austen and in the literature about her. There are illustrations of family, people and places associated with her, with many of the pieces cumulatively providing the foreground of her life. The beginnings are modest enough, for instance, in 1952, when nine of Jane Austen's music books were acquired by the Trustees, while in 1954 they obtained a needlecase which Jane had made and which she presented to her niece, Louisa Knight.

The accretion of scholarly records and critical appraisals begins to register in importance. The report for 1958 includes a piece of literary detection by John Gore which suggests that *Pride and Prejudice* influenced Emily Eden's conception of *The Semi-Attached Couple*, while the address in 1959 by E.G. Selwyn is on 'Jane Austen's Clergymen'. By 1961 an important critic, Andrew Wright, in 'Jane Austen from an American Viewpoint' defines her 'comic balance', and in 1962 Margaret Lane's address is full of good sense and perspective: 'What people think, what they say, how they feel and what they do, Jane Austen is scrupulous to tell us', but she leaves the background of it all to the reader generally. In successive years Elizabeth Jenkins and Lord David Cecil, major writers on Jane Austen, contributed pieces covering 'the aesthetic climate' in which she lived and an analysis of the minor works: both addresses provide evidence of Jane Austen's craftmanship, her care and dedication and capacity to rework material. Cecil asserts that 'her basic inspiration was comic', and that in her juvenilia her 'characteristic manner is present and formed'. L.P. Hartley, however, is impressed by the 'sadness to be found in all the novels, except perhaps in *Emma*'; John Bayley wisely notes that 'she uses the rigidity of society as a means of liberating her fancy and creative joy, whereas for later novelists the society they create is the product of their own interpretative and meaning-seeking vision'. 'Jane Austen and Charm' provided Elizabeth Bowen with a subject, with an informal and chatty rather than analytical approach. Rachel Trickett brings a sharpness of focus to bear on the nature of Jane Austen's comedy: 'Like all great comic artists she is under no illusion about the unresolved conflicts, the imperfection of life'. She gives particular attention to the combination of 'realism, morality and laughter' in *Pride and Prejudice.*

Between 1976 and 1985 the quality of these addresses to the Society is impressive, and I mean that without disrespect to the many other contributors to the Reports who found details of interest about Jane Austen and her life which enrich our appreciation of her. But the literary 'names' in the reports now take precedence, and they are mainstream literary names at that. David Gilson provides details on Sir Egerton Brydges, and later looks closely at the Oxford connections of the Austens and the system of 'founder's kin'. In 1977 the invaluable annual bibliography – modestly called 'Jane Austen Studies, 1977' is inaugurated, and Juliet McMaster considers 'Jane Austen and the Symptoms of Love' through some discriminating analysis of the subject: perhaps her most interesting emphasis here is on the fact that 'Some of the women in the novels are put to the pain of diagnosing the symptoms in the men they love themselves'. Marilyn Butler's paper in 1978 is especially stimulating on *Northanger Abbey,* which she calls 'a typical two-volume story, set out with a kind of blunt symmetry', with the first volume placed largely in Bath, and the second at Northanger. Lord David Cecil returns in 1979 with a 'A Summing Up' in which he draws particular attention to the fact that 'she realized what she could do and stuck to doing it'. Once again he places an uncompromising emphasis on the prevalence of the spirit of comedy in her work. Among other things, we are told, 'she reconciled reality with imagination', she possessed 'an insight into what is fundamental' and 'Her morality derived from her religion'.

Laurence Lerner's subject is 'Kissing', and so naturally probes the degree of physical contact between the lovers in the novels. He registers the evidence of strong feeling, but concludes that in *Sense and Sensibility*, for example, it produces 'not contact but separation'. There is certainly direct touching when Willoughby carries the injured Marianne into the parlour. He stresses that in the declaration scenes we are wrong if we are looking for an expression of sexual passion, instancing Wentworth and Anne when 'even at this moment of unsurpassable joy, the lovers obey that golden rule for successful lovers in Jane Austen: No Touching'.

Christopher Ricks is even more provocative: his 'Jane Austen and Mothering' opens in forthright parody with 'It is a half-truth universally acknowledged that Jane Austen disliked babies and didn't blankly like children. The other half-truth – that she sometimes loved babies and often loved children – is clear enough from her family life ...'. He stresses the teasing tone in the rest of the letter which contains the statement about Mrs Hall losing her baby because she happened to look at her husband. Unfortunately, one feels, too much of this address is spent sparring with the feminist critic Nina Auerbach.

A. Walton Litz, distinguished Jane Austen critic himself, marks his address by appealing to the general reader, something he maintains the best Jane Austen critics have always done. He also asserts that 'some of the most perceptive criticism has been produced by men and women working outside the academic establishment'. It is a bold and true statement to which these reports bear witness. The bulk of his fascinating lecture is devoted to *Pride and Prejudice* which, for him, and I suspect for many of us, is a fine blend of 'realism and romance'. He emphasizes that Jane Austen's small compass did not preclude her from producing 'great art'. He traces the village life which she described, contending that these small communities 'were microcosms of English society'. In fact, as he proves, she draws on 'the realities of a changing society'. Looked at critically, this is one of the best papers delivered to the Society, but the Reports themselves remain a microcosm of wider Jane Austen interests. Merely to read them through from the beginning is to be brought into contact with many of the details which made up a great writer's world. To echo A. Walton Litz's observation given above, she appeals both to the specialist and the general reader: I suggest that this is through the perfection of her art, the humanity of her comedy with its recognizable irony, the clearly enunciated morality embedded in ease of expression, rational control and structural coherence. The Society which bears her name is the natural home of the scholar, critic and enthusiast: and sometimes all three merge in its papers through the shared experience of her greatness.

There are so many reprints of Jane Austen's works that one needs to choose an annotated edition with a good critical introduction and textual/scholarly/period notes. *The Penguin English Library* opened its distinguished collection with a Jane Austen novel, *Persuasion*, a tribute in itself to her lasting appeal: the introduction is by D.W. Harding, of 'Regulated Hatred' celebrity, while those in succeeding volumes are by Jane Austen scholars and critics, for example, Tony Tanner (to *Sense and Sensibility, Pride and Prejudice* and *Mansfield Park*). These are both authoritative and stimulating, as we might expect, and have the merit of not talking down to the general reader and enthusiast who lacks an academic training. *The Oxford World's Classics* have recently reissued the novels, the volume containing *Northanger Abbey* also including *The Watsons, Lady Susan* and *Sanditon*, and there are newly commissioned introductions (1990) which embody up-to-date critical opinion. Oxford also kept in print the edition by R.W. Chapman, first issued in 1923 (the *Minor Works,* 1953), with a small number of later additions and corrections by Mary Lascelles. It is an excellent edition for, as Brian Southam has said when revising *Minor Works,* 'I have wanted to disturb as little as possible the style of editing and presentation which characterizes so distinctively R.W. Chapman's unobtrusive and scholarly attention to all the writings of Jane Austen'. Chapman's edition contains a splendid sense of period so essential to the study of this great writer.

This brief guide to important writers on Jane Austen follows a simple chronological line. Omissions do not mean rejection – most significant studies will be included in the Bibliography on pp. 129-37 – but merely reflect the severe prescription of space. My own views will be apparent from time to time interlinearly, but I hope, like Dr Chapman's editing, that they will never be obtrusive.

1

The Early Responses

In his introduction to *Jane Austen: The Critical Heritage*, vol. 1 (1968) Brian Southam, a distinguished scholar and critic of the novelist, observes that 'the birth and growth of Jane Austen's critical reputation was a dull and long-drawn-out affair'. He adds that 'There are no masterpieces of criticism in this volume'. Nevertheless it is stimulating to examine briefly what was said before the expansive developments which followed the publication of the *Memoir* in 1870. With it Jane Austen became 'dear Aunt Jane', in an irony which she would have appreciated, and it is in the same year that the Shakespearian scholar Richard Simpson evaluates the real quality of her achievement. He acclaims her as a genius, saying that she is 'remarkable for the power of irony with which she searches the conduct and values of her society' (Southam's words). He goes on to say that Simpson 'had no antecedents and no immediate following' – what he defines as her 'controlling irony' remained unrecognized for many years.

In her own lifetime and in a limited circle her novels 'enjoyed a reputation for their decorum, their realism and wit'. But *Mansfield Park*, to Jane Austen's disappointment, went unreviewed, though *Emma* (see later) moved Scott to a generous acknowledgement and partial investigation of the nature of her achievement. Yet the fact that she wrote about ordinary people was often seen as a limitation, even though her contemporary, Susan Ferrier, praised *Emma* in a letter

11

Jane Austen

written in 1816, by observing that 'the characters are all so true to life, and the style so piquant, that it does not require the adventitious aids of mystery and adventure'. But for the most part, Southam suggests that her contemporaries were not willing to accept 'her disconcerting account of the ways and values of their own society'.

Southam reasons that Jane Austen may well have been largely ignored during the period 1821-70 because of the sheer volume of reading material available. But with the publication of her novels in Bentley's standard edition (1833), the small, steady, and sometimes discriminating following begins to appear. Before that, the sparse appraisals inevitably contained plot summary and generalizations about character and situation. Thus, the writer in the *British Critic* (May 1812) noted (of *Sense and Sensibility*) that 'The characters are happily delineated and admirably sustained'. The writer also sees the moral mode of the writing, though somewhat sententiously, recording 'many sober and salutary maxims for the conduct of life'. The same journal was to find Mr Bennet 'a reserved, acute, and satirical, but indolent personage, who sees and laughs at the follies and indiscretions of his dependents, without making any exertions to correct them'. The *Critical Review* (March 1813) thought that Elizabeth was 'the *Beatrice* of the tale' on whose character 'the main interest of the novel depends', while 'The sentiments, which are dispersed over the work, do great credit to the *sense and sensibility* of the authoress'.

But it is Scott's unsigned review of *Emma* in the *Quarterly* (issued March 1816) which anticipates and asserts considered and serious evaluation of Jane Austen. Scott is bold and unequivocal. He says of her novels that 'They belong to a class of fictions which has arisen almost in our own times, and which draws the characters and incidents introduced more immediately from the current of ordinary life than was permitted by the former rules of the novel'. After tracing the novel as a descendant of romances, he defines the kind of fiction which has superseded the habits of romance and sentiment as 'a correct and striking representation of that which is daily taking place ...'. He says that Jane Austen 'has produced sketches of such spirit and originality...her dramatis personae conduct themselves upon the motives and principles which the readers may recognize as ruling their own and that of most of their own acquaintances'. Plot summaries of *Sense and Sensibility* and *Pride and Prejudice* are followed by acute particularities: he notes the 'force and precision' which characterizes the drawing of Mr Bennet and that 'servile young sprig of divinity', Mr Collins. *Emma* is his main focus: she is the 'princess paramount', and her 'entanglements bring on only a train of mistakes and embarassing situations... in which the author displays her peculiar powers of humour and knowledge of human life'. He follows this with an interesting analogy: 'The author's knowledge of the world, and the peculiar tact with which she presents characters that the reader cannot fail to recognize, reminds us of something of the merits of the Flemish school of painting'. He also notes the 'neatness and point' of the narrative and the 'quiet yet comic dialogue'. Scott's great merit is that his eye is always on the novel, though one feels that he fails to grasp the full ironic realism of the presentation of Mr Woodhouse and Miss Bates, of whom he says they 'are ridiculous when first presented, but if too often brought forward or too long dwelt upon, their prosing is apt to become as tiresome in fiction as in real society'. One is tempted to agree, and to note it as an important stress in Jane Austen's realism.

The *Gentleman's Magazine* (September 1816) gives *Emma* a social habitation and a name: 'it delineates with great accuracy the habits and manners of a middle class of gentry; and of the inhabitants of a country village at one degree of rank and gentility beneath them', but notes also that 'It is amusing, if not instructive; and has no tendency to deteriorate the heart', the last phrase itself showing an amusing fear of the influence of fiction. After Jane Austen's death (18 July 1817) critical comment continues in the direct appraisal of the two posthumously published novels, *Northanger Abbey* and *Persuasion*. In an unsigned notice in the *British Critic* (December 1817) there is praise for Jane Austen's use of dialogue together with a recognition of 'her remarkable talent for observation; no ridiculous phrase, no affected sentiment, no

foolish pretension seems to escape her notice'. This insight is
followed by the assertion that she never employs satire, that
although she forces us to recognize our own absurdities her
works are really a species of 'good-humoured pleasantry'
which do not depend upon 'the interest of a narrative'. Acute-
ness and limitation of appraisal are mixed: *Persuasion*, we
are told, is a recommendation that 'young people should
always marry according to their own inclinations and upon
their own judgement'.

The most perceptive criticism published in the early years
after her death is that of Richard Whately in the *Quarterly*
(January 1821). He draws parallels with Maria Edgeworth,
and says that Jane Austen is religious without making religion obtrusive. He notes that the 'moral lessons...spring incidentally from the circumstances of the story', further
asserting that they are of the 'unpretending kind of instruction which is furnished by real life'. Nor is structure neglected, for there is a 'compactness of plan and unity of
action', and there are no 'extraordinary accidents'. In raising
the function of criticism himself, Whately is stating that the
novel is a serious art form: he even wonders 'whether Miss
Austen ever had access to the precepts of Aristotle; but there
are very few, if any, writers of fiction who have illustrated
them more successfully'. Whately's eye and ear cannot be
overpraised: he notices that 'the minute fidelity of detail, and
air of unstudied ease in the scenes presented...give fiction
the perfect appearance of reality'. Jane Austen's recording of
'private conversations and uncommunicated feelings' is balanced by her literary tact, her 'saying as little as possible in
her own person'. She is compared to Shakespeare for 'Like
him, she shows as admirable a discrimination in the characters of fools as of people of sense'. Whately's evaluations are
never dull: he says that Sir Thomas Bertram exerts wise
judgement when given the facts of a situation, but that he is
one of those men 'who are quite destitute of actuteness of
discernment and adroitness of conduct', further testimony to
the imaginative accuracy of Jane Austen's presentation. *Persuasion* is singled out for special praise.

Scott had not finished. His celebrated self-judgement is set beside a generous acknowledgement which must be quoted in any early reception of Jane Austen:

> The Big Bow-wow strain I can do myself like any now going, but the exquisite touch which renders ordinary commonplace things and characters interesting from the truth of the description and the sentiment is denied to me. What a pity such a gifted creature died so early.

Journal of Sir Walter Scott
14 March 1826

Four years later, in the *Edinburgh Review* of July 1830, the early notes of future greatness are sounded: the writer observes of Jane Austen's readers that 'She was too natural for them', going on to explain that 'They did not consider that the highest triumph of art consists in its concealment', that 'Her forte consists not so much in describing events, as in drawing characters', and here she is unsurpassed. This perception embraces the dialogue and its inherent humour, though the word irony is not mentioned: 'A nicely-regulated vein of humour runs though her writings, never breaking out into broad mirth', and this is accompanied by the 'purest morality, undeviating good sense'.

The next, almost extreme, laudatory statement is that of Macaulay, who wrote in the *Edinburgh Review* (January 1843, pp. 561-2) that she approached more closely the manner of Shakespeare, her characters being 'all as perfectly discriminated from each other as if they were the most eccentric of human beings'. Four years later, G.H. Lewes wrote in *Fraser's* (December 1847) that 'Fielding and Miss Austen are the greatest novelists in our language', soon engaging with Charlotte Brontë, who read his review and rejected his judgement, writing to him that Jane Austen commanded 'no open country, no fresh air, no blue hill, no bonny beck'. Comparing Jane Austen to George Sand, she says that the latter 'is sagacious and profound; Miss Austen is only shrewd and observant' (12 January 1848). In a later letter she denied the greatness of Jane Austen because of her lack of poetry, while to W.S. Williams she wrote on 12th April 1850 'there is a Chinese fidelity, a miniature delicacy in the painting: she ruffles her reader by nothing vehement, disturbs him by nothing profound: the Passions are perfectly unknown to her; she rejects even a speaking acquaintance with that stormy Sisterhood; even to the Feelings she vouchsafes no more than an occasional grateful but distant recognition'. It is a subjective and feeling response, indicating a lack of sympathetic perception and affinity. From *Sense and Sensibility* onwards the feelings are central to Jane Austen's conception, and the passions, though regulated by the balanced prose, surface dangerously within characters. Marianne has impetuous feelings and thwarted passions, though the last word would not be in her vocabulary. We think of the passion of Darcy and his feeling rejection by Elizabeth, or we measure Emma's suppressed feeling as she compounds her errors before coming to a feeling self-recognition. Jane Austen's 18th-century reading inheritance put the rational stamp on her style, but part of her extraordinary achievement is seen in her ability to convey deep feeling through civilised and stringent discipline. With her, gentility is not synonymous with emotional insensibility; it is rather that she exposes, subtly and ironically, the human, warm responses below the polite veneer which hides them in society.

By the mid-19th century Jane Austen's particular strengths were beginning to be noticed. A writer in the *New Monthly Magazine* (May 1852) praised her 'commonplace people', adding that 'we never miss the excitation which depends upon a narrative of uncommon events'. The success of her novels depends upon her 'unaffected good sense, her shrewd insight, her felicitous irony, and the fruitful harvest of her quiet eye', while she manages to avoid 'the manner of the sententious teacher'. In the *Westminster Review* (July 1852) Lewes said that 'To read one of her books is like an actual experience of life'. It was in 1859 that Lewes offered what Southam heads as 'The great appraisal'. A complete article is devoted to her in *Blackwood's* (July 1859). Among the points Lewes makes is that she survives reading aloud, and that Fielding is 'inferior to her, we think, in real humour'.

He stresses rightly the 'economy of art' and again underlines the realism – 'We never tire of her characters. They become equal to actual experience'. There is praise too for her dramatic presentation, while 'the construction of her stories is admirable'. Her limitations are seen in the lack of description of her characters, and 'the absence of all sense of outward world'. There are also deficiencies 'in poetry and passion', and though she has 'but an indifferent story to tell', the art of her narration is 'incomparable'. Although Lewes rates Jane Austen highly, his own criticism shows serious deficiencies in intellectual and imaginative appraisal: 'There are neither epigrams nor aphorisms, neither subtle analyses nor eloquent descriptions. She is without grace or felicity of expression; she has neither fervid nor philosophic comment. Her charm lies solely in the art of representing life and character, and that is exquisite.' The denials are neither convincing nor absolute: they reflect, in fact, an inability to read closely or to adduce the perfection of utterance which is itself epigrammatic, eloquent and felicitous. Great claims have been made on behalf of Lewes' criticism: his remarks on Jane Austen reveal a limited and unenlightened perspective: 'Such art as hers can never grow old, never be superseded. But, after all, miniatures are not frescoes, and her works are miniatures. Her place is among the Immortals; but the pedestal is erected in a quiet niche of the great temple.' The sound of this is more than the matter, the prose makes images, but the eye has been withdrawn from the text.

W.F. Pollock's praise (*Fraser's*, January 1860) also suggests limitations, though he recognizes that Jane Austen always keeps to the society which she knows well. His comments, however, do embrace the 'good English, the same refined style, the same simplicity and truth' as well as her 'unapproachable' dramatic representation. This tendency to regard her area as prescribed and therefore inhibiting is seen in a letter from Edward Fitzgerald to Pollock (24 December 1871) where he observes 'She is capital as far as she goes: but she never goes out of the Parlour'.

Southam rightly praises Julia Kavanagh's neglected study of Jane Austen in her *English Women of Letters* (1862,

pp. 251-74). She focuses initially on the 'reality' of Jane
Austen's characterization, and defines this directly – 'She
cannot be said to have created or invented; Jane Austen had
an infinitely rarer gift – she saw'. In this fine chapter there
are anticipations of 20th-century critical stances, seen in
recognitions such as her having 'a touch so fine that we often
do not perceive its severity'. Jane Austen knew what to
withhold as well as what to say, and she is unequalled in a
'wide' region, 'the region of commonplaces'. There is a positive
refreshment in coming across statements such as 'delicate
irony is her keenest weapon'. This is followed by penetrating
analyses of character, though Miss Kavanagh says that the
author does 'not analyse her characters, they speak for themselves'. She adds 'They talk as people talk in the world, and
quietly betray their inner being in their folly, falsehood, or
assumption'. Yet Julia Kavanagh registers a supposed weakness: it is that 'everything is told in the same tone'.

With George Eliot at the height of her fame, and certainly
influenced by her re-readings of Jane Austen, in particular,
Emma, it was perhaps inevitable that E.S. Dallas, reviewing
Felix Holt in the *Times*, should compare the two novelists and
elevate George Eliot at the expense of Jane Austen. Nonetheless the latter comes in for some shrewd analysis, as in

> Nothing can be more natural than the way in which she
> evolves an event, leading up to it with the clearest motives
> and the most likely accidents, never saying too much, never
> too little, nothing too soon, nothing too late, sparing of reflec-
> tion, and letting her characters speak for themselves.

26 June 1866

The writer in the *Englishwoman's Domestic Magazine* (July,
August 1866) praises Jane Austen's 'observation, insight,
taste, humour, and good sense; the rest was cultivation'. The
ethical direction follows – 'she wrote to amuse, not to in-
struct, but she took care to write nothing that should not have
an instructive tendency. She might be called a moral homoeo-
path; not having the power or desire to give strong doses, she

administered her physic in such diluted form, that the pleasant medium in which it was conveyed was much more wholesome and no less palatable'. Miss Bates is thought to be '*too natural*', while the return of Fanny to Portsmouth 'is the greatest social contrast to be found in any of her books'. The running emphasis, which takes in satire, irony and wit, finds Jane Austen inevitably good-natured, an interesting contrast with the direction taken in some mid-20th-century criticism. But the economic basis of marriage is also noted – 'Her love is nothing more rash than a deep attachment based on esteem, a chastened affection which does not catch fire under a thousand a year'. Her great deficiency, apparently, lies in the fact that none of her characters is likeable.

Mrs Oliphant (*Blackwood's*, March 1870) reviewed the *Memoir*, noting in Jane Austen 'the fine vein of feminine cynicism', the 'subtle, delicate, speculative temper' which makes her characterization 'so refined and so trenchant, so softly feminine and polite, and so true'. Mrs Oliphant remarks on the 'consistent, remorseless ridicule' contained in the portrait of Mr Collins, a portrait which is 'amazing in its unity and completeness.... It is, we repeat, cruel in its perfection'. The writer in *St Paul's Magazine* (March 1870) says that Jane Austen is 'true in conception and faultless in execution', and that 'Her just sense of proportion never deserts her'. She is always conscious of propriety, and we can appreciate 'a pleasant vein of irony' which runs thoughout her novels; she knew 'her own boundaries'. Despite this, the writer attacks Elizabeth Bennet for her 'vulgarity' and also for her 'vanity and self-satisfaction', for Jane Austen's 'special power lay in the satire of the mean and the ridiculous'.

Southam rightly stresses the primacy of Richard Simpson in this period of Jane Austen criticism (*North British Review*, April 1870). Simpson observes 'She began by being an ironical critic...imitating and exaggerating the faults of her models, thus clearing the fountain by first stirring the mud'. Simpson's appreciation is enhanced by his own style, which at times complements Jane Austen's as in 'the subtle humour, the fine sense of the incongruous, the constant presence and alertness of mind'. He refers to her lack of poetry, adding that she displays an 'habitual exaltation of judgement over passion, of the spiritual over the poetical and imaginative faculties'. His own emphasis is on the 'manifest irony of her whole mass of compositions'. Simpson states that she is a humorist, but underlines her kindliness; the thoroughness of her method and the supreme awareness of man as a social being typify her work. Her sense of structure is evident throughout – 'What she wrote was worked up by incessant labour into its perfect form'. On the other hand, he asserts that 'She wrote her first novel with a polemical bias against the sudden flush of love'. This must be seen as a simplification when one considers the accretion of sympathy for Marianne and a running sub-text which demonstrates that reason alone is inadequate in the unexpected situations of life. Simpson, however, traces the progression from the fools of farce to the rather more complex presentation of Mr Woodhouse, and he links style and propriety in crisp statement and analogy; 'She is neat, epigrammatic, and incisive, but always a lady; there is no brandy and cayenne in her farrago'.

Simpson is perhaps the most penetrating critic of the first period of Jane Austen appraisal, though his emphasis does tend to the 'kindly'. We are aware then that there is much stimulating individual appreciation, but rarely any detailed and coherent line of argument. Early critics of the novel in the 19th century, having generous space in their particular journals, used the descriptive mode – the often lengthy plot summary, the leisured analogy with the works of another writer, and the facile generalization. This meant that the eye was not always on the text, that contemporary fashions of appraisal conditioned judgements and that, as Southam says, the emergence of the massive Victorian novels where much happened led to a delay in the full and informed response which Jane Austen merits. Nevertheless there is real value in contemporary and following registers: taken as a whole they provide us with a perspective on a great writer before that writer is subjected to the disciplines and sophistications of scholarship and criticism.

2

Reticence and Reputation: Early Biography

The *Biographical Notice of the Author*, issued in 1818 with *Persuasion* and *Northanger Abbey*, and written by Henry Austen, is the starting point for investigation. The tone of it, however, is bland and cloying. Can we believe that 'she never deserved disapprobation' and that in her family 'she never met reproof'? She was of unfailing goodwill, and given to 'A life of usefulness, literature and religion'. There is much on her 'personal attractions'; we are told of her features that 'Their assemblage produced an unrivalled expression of that cheerfulness, sensibility, and benevolence, which were her real characteristics', and of her personality, that 'she was formed for elegant and rational society'. She also enjoyed dancing and was an accomplished musician. She lacked affectation and never commented unkindly on others, and 'She never uttered either a hasty, a silly, or a severe expression. In short, her temper was as polished as her wit'. She read aloud well, was not desirous of fame and certainly not of publicity, while 'At an early age she was enamoured of Gilpin on the Picturesque; and she seldom changed her opinions either on books or men'. Her evaluations of the great writers of the 18th century are given, and with regard to Fielding we are told that 'she recoiled from everything gross. Neither nature, wit, nor humour, could make her amends for so very low a scale of morals'. Austen asserts that she drew

from nature but 'never from individuals'. Finally, her intense
piety is stressed, the last words of the original notice being
'her opinions accorded strictly with those of the Established
Church'. How this paragon came to write the novels she did
we shall never know: the claustrophobic respectability shuts
her off from the readers who have come to appreciate not
merely the wit and wisdom but also the deft touches of ironic
malice which inform her work. There is no hint here of *Lady
Susan*, and one feels that suppression has more than a touch
of hypocrisy about it. But moral reputation is all, and brevity
here is the soul of discretion.

The *Memoir* of 1870 by her nephew J.E. Austen-Leigh is
warm and unashamedly derived from personal recollections
of the last phase of Jane Austen's life. The emphasis is on her
uneventful life and sweet nature: 'kind, sympathising and
amusing'. There follows a history of Jane's immediate ancestors, her brothers and the family generally, all in considerable detail. The major stress, as we have come to expect (but
remember that it would be fresh in 1870) is on the loving
relationship with her sister Cassandra. There is a sound
account of the fashions and manners of the period, much of
it of great social interest. There is also some engaging frank-
ness: ch. 3, for instance, opens with the words 'I know little
of Jane Austen's childhood'. Austen-Leigh reproduces, however, her very early work 'The Mystery', and explores the
character of Mrs Lefroy, who died in 1804 and was commem-
orated by Jane some four years later, in verse which is
undistinguished and mannered. A sequence of letters to
Cassandra show Jane Austen's powers of observation and her
ability to convey snippets of news in a racy way. Chawton is
described almost poetically by Austen-Leigh, who then deals
with Jane Austen's range of reading and the reminiscences
of her by nephews and nieces. Her own letters, and extracts
from them, provide plenty of wit and sparkle, as in 'So Miss
B. is actually married, but I have never seen it in the papers;
and one may as well be single if the wedding is not to be in
print'.

Austen-Leigh says that he will 'not venture to speak of her
religious principles: that is a subject on which she herself was

more inclined to *think* and *act* than to *talk*... ', an interesting reticence in view of the statements in the *Biographical Notice*. But he does note the inspiration that the move to Chawton brought with it. Consequently the latter part of her life is covered in some detail with the supplement of the letters, and includes the journeys Jane Austen made to London. The fact that she was secluded from the mainstream of the literary world is stressed, and the anecdote of the verger at Winchester Cathedral wanting to know 'whether there was anything particular about that lady; so many people want to know where she was buried?' is given. The correspondence with Mr Clarke, the Prince Regent's librarian, together with the effect of this royal notice on her, bulks large. Writing in 1869, Austen-Leigh is able to comment on the 'slow-growth' of Jane Austen's 'literary reputation'. In addition, he traces her efforts to get her works published, deducing that a version of *Pride and Prejudice* 'was declined by return of post' in November 1797. He refers to Whately's review of 1821, and also quotes Sir Egerton Brydges' praise – 'Her novels are more true to nature, and have, for my sympathies, passages of finer feeling than any others of this age'. Many tributes are cited before Austen-Leigh makes his own observations on the novels. He particularly admires her portraits of the clergy, and considers that 'The characters of the John Dashwoods, Mr Collins, and the Thorpes stand out from the canvas with a vigour and originality which cannot be surpassed'. He finds in the later works, however, 'a deeper insight into the delicate anatomy of the human heart'.

Her final years, with the onset of her illness and, despite this, her fortitude and working powers in adversity, are recorded with sympathetic insight. The cancelled chapter of *Persuasion* is given in full, and extracts from *Sanditon*, as he says, illustrate that here her characters 'are at least original and unlike any that the author had produced before'. The postscript refers to the destruction of family letters and papers which would have enabled him to write a fuller biography; he was forced to draw upon his own recollections, and his conclusions are not dissimilar from those given in the *Biographical Notice*:

There was in her nothing eccentric or angular; no ruggedness
of temper; no singularity of manner; none of the morbid
sensibility of exaggeration of feeling, which not unfrequently
accompanies great talents, to be worked up into a picture.
Hers was a mind well balanced on a basis of good sense,
sweetened by an affectionate heart, and regulated by fixed
principles....

Fifty-two years on from that first notice there is a fuller
outline, but no change.

    Jane Austen: Her Life and Letters: A Family Record (1913)
by William Austen-Leigh and Richard Arthur Austen-Leigh
is the major biographical landmark between the *Memoir* of
1870-1 and Elizabeth Jenkins' study in 1938. It draws on the
Brabourne *Letters* between Jane and Cassandra (1884) and
also takes into account Constance Hill's *Jane Austen: Her
Home and Her Friends* (1902) which gives both family tradi-
tions and topographical information. The authors feel that
the *Memoir* 'needs to be supplemented' because of its limited
perspective of nephews and nieces who were close to their
aunt at a particular time and 'were not likely to be the
recipients of her inmost confidences on the wants and sentiments of her youth'. They maintain that 'the emotional and
romantic side of her nature – a very real one – has not been
dwelt upon'. They also feel that it has not been fully appreciated just how much she had gone into society, and that her
life was not as uneventful as has so often been claimed. Their
method is 'intended as a narrative, and not as a piece of
literary criticism'. What it means in practice is that long
quotations from the letters – and from some written by other
members of the family – are interlined with commentary
which is at once authoritative, responsible and, often,
smoothly persuasive in endorsing the moderate view.

    Minor errors in the *Memoir* are corrected, the first Steven-
ton years are attractively covered, while the beauty of the
hedgerows there are connected with Jane Austen's descriptions in, for example, *Persuasion*. George Austen's letter to
his sister of 17th December 1775 records the birth of the
novelist the previous day: 'We now have another girl, a

present plaything for her sister Cassy, and a future companion. She is to be Jenny...'. From time to time there is inter-
polative comment on the adult writer, though it is generally
cautious, such as 'she probably shared the feeling of moderate Toryism which prevailed in her family'.

The traumatic effect of the execution of the Comte de
Feuillide (22 February 1794) is recorded. His wife Eliza's
continuing close links with the Austens probably meant that
the tragedy 'haunted Jane's memory for a long time to come'.
Equally, the Steventon theatricals are seen as a stimulating
and productive influence on her emergent writing. The
Austen-Leighs are especially interesting in what they say
about *Lady Susan*. The author of the *Memoir* apparently did
not wish to have it published (it was issued with the *Memoir*
in error, they say), but they consider that 'Strictly speaking,
it is not a story but a study'. It is also a story, but their
assessment is worth quoting: 'It is equally remarkable that
an inexperienced girl should have had independence and
boldness enough to draw at full length a woman of the type
of Lady Susan, and that, after she had done so, the purity of
her imagination and the delicacy of her taste, should have
prevented her from ever repeating the experiment'. The tone
and the conclusion betray that curious mixture of acknowledgement and deliberately blinkered emphasis. Her reading
alone would have given her the inspiration for *Lady Susan*,
while the dubious use of 'purity' looks back to the paragon of
the *Memoir*, of whom one of her nieces observed, 'I do not
suppose she ever in her life said a sharp thing' (a strange
thing to say, for she certainly did in her novels).

The authors, however, boldly trace the romances of her life,
printing her letter to her brother Frank about Blackall's
marriage to Miss Lewis with its acid, sharp comments. They
dismiss as 'impossible' the meeting with a young man on a
trip to Switzerland, considering the trip impossible too. Another important section is the one which deals with Mr
Austen's sudden decision to move to Bath. Here they reject
another romance rumoured with one of the Digweed
brothers. At the same time they admit that Cassandra's
burning of her sister's letters after her death 'was a proof of

their emotional interest'.

The close examination of the manuscript of *The Watsons* at least has the beginnings of scholarship:

> All the pages are written in her beautifully neat handwriting, but some seem to flow on without doubt or difficulty, while others are subject to copious corrections. As all the MSS of her six published novels have perished, it is worth our while to notice her methods where we can.

The chapter on Southampton and Chawton covers the death of Edward's wife, and refers to a missing letter between October 15th and 24th 1808 in which he must have offered his mother the cottage at Chawton, perhaps wishing 'to bind his mother and sisters more closely to himself'. The Austen-Leighs focus sensitively on this period (1808-9), sensing Jane Austen's discouragement at having written three novels, all unpublished; they note her determined attempt in April 1809 to get *Lady Susan* accepted.

We are always aware of the care, of the dedicated determination to get things right about the authoress, to print the letters and extracts in a chronological sequence. But there are some departures in the manner of the modern biographer who makes deduction synonymous with fact. Here is their subject in 1809: 'Jane Austen was now between thirty-three and thirty-four years old. She was absolutely free from any artistic self-consciousness, from any eccentricity of either temper or manner'. It is an assured statement intent on preserving the even image. Fulsome quotations from the *Memoir* succeed this, with physical description and moral quality always evident. She was also good at games, being 'invincible' at cup-and-ball and spillikins. By 1811 we are told that 'Since her fit of youthful enthusiasm, when she had composed three stories in little more than three years, she had had much experience of life to sober and strengthen her'. The implication here is that because of the 'experience of life' she made extensive revisions to the novels she had written.

From then on there are some passing comments between the letters which are of interest. One of her letters to her brother Frank is analysed: according to the Austen-Leighs it shows her 'strong preference for remaining unknown if she could, and the invariable sweetness of temper which forbade her to blame a brother whom she loved because he had made such concealment impossible'. There are some neat comments on *Mansfield Park* ('the decorous, though somewhat cold dignity of Sir Thomas Bertram's household'): the authors feel strongly that Fanny's brother William is drawn from life – 'She must, one would think, have had in mind her brother Charles'. They also feel that Jane Austen's health began to deteriorate as a result of nursing her brother Henry during his serious illness in October 1815. They publish her collection of 'Opinions of *Emma*' (the capacity to laugh at herself evident from some of the adverse comments) and the fascinating 'plan of a novel'.

There is a warm account of her as an aunt in her last years. The Austen-Leighs feel that her comments on marriage reflect her candour, and select the kindness in her appraisal of Anna Lefroy's writing and the quality of her practical advice. These show her disciplined approach to her own art. They point out her optimism about her health, and then there is the fragment of *Sanditon*, where they feel 'there is little of the subtle refinement which we are accustomed to associate with her work, and certainly nothing of the tender sentiment of *Persuasion*'. There is an appendix on the texts of the novels, with a number of errors spotted and corrected, and there is a useful bibliography up to 1913. The book is dated and has been superseded by the publication of the *Letters*, but it remains a quarry and a clear account in its own right.

3

The Emergent Classic

In his Introduction to *Jane Austen: The Critical Heritage*, vol. 2 (1987), Brian Southam draws attention to the fact that the two editions of the *Memoir* in 1870-1 called forth a total of seventeen reviews. He stresses the tone of '*patronising* admiration' which appears when the novels are mentioned, or the 'rhapsodical pulsations, syrupy apostrophisings and gaspings of delight' with which Anne Thackeray referred to the 'Dear books' in the *Cornhill Magazine* in 1871. At the same time he acknowledges that she shows a positive insight into the nature of Jane Austen's writing, though she was responsible for establishing a cloying tradition. A writer in 1897 considered that the word which summed her up was 'delightful', but before that, in 1876, Leslie Stephen had commented on the 'popularity of Miss Austen' in an unsigned article in the *Cornhill Magazine*. He refers to 'Austenolatry' and, while allowing her considerable achievement 'within her own sphere', asserts that he would reject the idea 'that she was therefore entitled to be ranked with the great authors who have sounded the depths of human passion, or found symbols for the finest speculations of the human intellect, instead of amusing themselves with the humours of a country tea-table' (I found this a little patronizing). He finds the nature of her humour is 'drawn so excessively mild', and this accounts in part for her popularity, for 'there is not a single flash of biting satire'. Stephen sounds a note which has become part of a 20th-century critical lobby: 'The harsh hideous facts with which ninety-nine out of a hundred of our fellow-creatures are constantly struggling, are never admitted into this delightful world of well-warmed county houses'. This tame Jane Austen is diminished by implication: the failure here is to measure universal truths. She wrote about what she knew, and there is no suggestion in Stephen's assessment that her wisdom is of any account.

George Pellew's *Jane Austen's Novels* (1883) is criticism of a very different order, for he attempts to place her historically, and to estimate the influences of the past and the present which made her the writer she was. He refers to her 'truth to nature, and such witty discrimination of character'. He also praises her accuracy, asserting that 'She anticipated the scientific precision that the spirit of the age is now demanding in literature and art'. He refers to Zola and Whitman in his own time, and anticipates the nature of realism to come. He finds Jane Austen's characters natural, clearly differentiated, and none of them caricatures. Strangely, however, he says that her descriptions are from the outside, and that she does not provide us with 'an insight into their principles of action, their thoughts and feelings. She has not, perhaps, the power of projecting herself into a character, and becoming that character for the time'. This, of course, ignores the subtlety of identification with the heroines. Pellew, however, singles out the 'natural ease and appropriateness of the conversations', rightly stressing the mastery that is shown not only, for example, in Miss Bates, but also in the exchanges between Catherine Morland and Isabella. But 'charm' is one of the stressed qualities – 'we become conscious of the charm of one of the wittiest and brightest women that ever lived'. Pellew has his own insights, though 'the petty inconsistencies and social vanities of human beings are as enduring as their more impressive qualities; and it is of these that Miss Austen writes...'. Pellew's commentary is a mixture of fine analysis and integral evaluation; in a letter addressed to him Henry James refers to 'the extraordinary vividness with which she saw what she did see' and then reveals his own failure at fuller comprehension by saying that her heroines 'had undoubtedly small and second-rate minds and were perfect little she-Philistines'. Although he allows that this makes them interesting, he says that 'All that there was of them was feeling – a sort of simple undistracted concentrated feeling which we scarcely find any more'. This is qualified by the assertion that Emma and Anne Elliot 'give us as great an impression of "passion"... as the ladies of G. Sand and Balzac'. There is some truth in this but the perspective is wrong.

In 1890 Goldwin Smith published his *Jane Austen* in the 'Great Writers' series. He believes tht there are no 'fine things to be said about Jane Austen...nothing calling in any way for elaborate interpretation'. His assertion is that 'Her genius is shown in making the familiar and commonplace intensely interesting and amusing'. He feels that there is little to distinguish the early novels from the late novels, but in praising her commonplace presentation he introduced, like Stephen before him, a moral note into his appraisal: 'Few sets of people, perhaps, ever did less for humanity or exercised less influence on its progress than the denizens of Mansfield Park and Pemberley, Longbourn and Hartfield, in Jane Austen's day'. They are 'the lightest of bubbles', 'made bright for ever by the genius of Jane Austen'.

W.D. Howells champions Jane Austen's realism in *Criticism and Fiction* (1891), referring to 'the simple verity, the refined perfection of Miss Austen', but he also indulges in uncritical worship of 'the divine Jane and her novels'. He says 'She was great and they were beautiful, because she and they were honest, and dealt with nature nearly a hundred years ago as realism deals with it today'. She treated her material 'with entire truthfulness', and this is what Howells defines as realism. As far as Howells is concerned, the great writers who succeeded her succumbed to the 'mania of romanticism' and were unable to escape 'the taint of their time'. It is apparent from this that Howells lacked critical perspective and sharpness. His was an early subscription to the Janeite tradition, a kind of 'mania of romanticism' which regularly occurs later in writings about her.

In her *Points of View* (1891) Agnes Repplier praises the lightness of Jane Austen's touch in her portraits of clergymen (the comparison is with those of Charlotte Brontë). She finds her tolerant and good-natured towards her foolish or unlikeable characters. Jane Austen's work has 'a fine, thin perfection' (rather like Agnes Repplier's style) which 'appeals to the mature observation of men and women'. Later, in her *Essays in Miniature* (1892), she probes more deeply, writing about how she [Jane Austen] 'reveals to us with merciless distinctness the secret springs that move the human heart'. The concentration here is on conversation in Jane Austen's novels, and how the characters 'stand convicted' once they open their mouths. Everything that Mrs Norris says contains 'a new and luminous revelation', and Miss Repplier singles out for attention the second chapter of *Sense and Sensibility*, where the conversation betrays 'the feeble egotism of Mr Dashwood, and the adroit meanness of his spouse'. But other emphases in Miss Repplier's work are odd, as in her essay in *The Critic* (December 1900), where she says that although the taste and humour of the novels is never in doubt, they are 'destitute of passion'.

George Saintsbury wrote a preface to *Pride and Prejudice* in 1894 in which he unequivocally expresses his preference for it – 'the most perfect, the most characteristic, the most eminently quintessential of its author's works'. He goes on to define her humour, referring to its 'demureness, extreme minuteness of touch, avoidance of loud tones and glaring effects'. He acknowledges that there is too, though it is expressed in a refined way, 'an insatiable and ruthless delight in roasting and cutting up a fool'. He feels that this capacity contributed largely to her artistic sense. There is singular praise for the depiction of Mr Collins – 'alive, imperishable, more real than hundreds of prime ministers and archbishops...' and a fine indication of the range of Jane Austen's critical survey of 'eighteenth-century humanity, its Philistinism, its well-meaning but hide-bound morality, its formal pettiness, its grovelling respect for rank, its materialism, its selfishness', all exemplified in the persona of Mr Collins. Although Elizabeth is not outwardly passionate, Saintsbury sees her as a full and striking character who, fortunately for him, exhibits nothing of the 'New Woman'.

Henry James also contributes to the developing appraisals of Jane Austen. In 'The Lesson of Balzac' (1905) he indicates 'her light felicity' and then gets lost in a welter of imagery supposedly descriptive of her popularization by the book-trade, who have found her 'so infinitely to their material purpose'. His own explanation of this in critical terms is to note 'the extraordinary grace of her facility, in fact of her unconsciousness'. The tone is condescending at best, though he does acknowledge her 'little touches of human truth, little glimpses of steady vision, little master-strokes of imagination'. Serious evaluation of Jane Austen, as has often been said, begins with A.C. Bradley's lecture on her, printed in *Essays and Studies* in 1911. He is unashamedly a Janeite who assumes that he is talking to the 'faithful'. Again we meet the analogy with Shakespeare, though Bradley modestly says that he is merely offering a few notes on Jane Austen's writing. He believes that 'There are two distinct strains in Jane Austen. She is a moralist and a humorist', and that these strains are often found together in her works. She observes human nature, like Johnson before her, with 'penetration' and 'complete honesty'. She resists 'speculation' and rejects sentiment. She also refuses to 'express a deeper concern than she feels for misfortune or grief, and with both there is an occasional touch of brutality in the manner of the refusal'.

He feels that her morality, while part of the substance of her writing, is also 'openly expressed' on occasions. Her 'abstract titles' reflect 'the movement of her mind' and her heroines such as Elinor, Fanny and Anne have her approval, doing 'the right thing, however disagreeable or prosaic it may be'. But in the case of the first two he feels that 'the suppression of feeling and fancy' reduces their 'charm' (we note the use of the word yet again). She does not 'depict those conflicts of violent passions', and always avoids what she does not know. Because of this 'her novels make exceptionally peaceful reading', and he feels that 'she was blessed with a sunny temper'. She avoids the danger of 'falsifying nature' by her 'moralising tendency' and Bradley feels that 'her sympathies and antipathies never make her unjust', citing

Mrs Norris' final dedication to Maria as evidence of this. He defines her attitude towards her characters as one of 'ironical amusement, because they never see the situation as it really is and as she sees it'. *Emma* is much praised, Mr Woodhouse and Miss Bates both 'being the object equally of our laughter and our unqualified respect and affection'. Bradley is here, I think, direct and simple, and it could be argued that they are equally the object of our irritation, our criticism and our compassion. Bradley, to a limited extent, is appreciative, but only period criticism like his could consider Mr Woodhouse 'next to Don Quixote, perhaps the most perfect gentleman in fiction'. However, his general appraisal of *Emma* is a well-reasoned one: 'Most of the characters are involved in the contrast of reality and illusion, but it is concentrated on Emma'. Bradley describes the characterization in *Mansfield Park* as 'exceptionally delicate and subtle' and perhaps unusually for this time, he applies the above phrase particularly to Fanny Price. *Mansfield Park* is 'superior to the youthful work, and superior in some degree to *Emma* and *Persuasion*'. Much is gained from repeated readings of *Mansfield Park*; in singling out its complexity, maturity and artistic form, Bradley is anticipating here much later 20th-century criticism.

In the *Victorian Age in Literature* (1913) G.K. Chesterton emphasizes her salient achievements, recognizing 'the complete common sense' of her attitudes and expression. One of her great strengths was that she knew and understood men (one would think this a large claim), Chesterton citing as evidence Darcy's acknowledgement of his own faults. In a fine turn of phrase he observes 'Jane Austen may have been protected from truth: but it was precious little of truth that was protected from her'.

Virginia Woolf's remarks in the *TLS* of 8th May 1913 place Jane Austen in the first three among the great English novelists, and note 'the slow and very steady rise of her reputation'. For Virginia Woolf, to re-read Jane Austen is to be exalted, but she feels that the defects should be acknowledged 'by readers who are as candid as Jane Austen herself would wish them to be'. She feels that there is 'too little of the rebel in her composition.... She seems at times to have accepted life too calmly as she found it, and to any one who reads her biography or letters it is plain that life showed her a great deal that was smug, commonplace, and, in a bad sense of the word, artificial'. True, but one would surely say that it was this material which provided her with her fiction and with the moral perspective with which she informs it. Virginia Woolf believes that Jane Austen accepts her world as well as laughing at it, 'and that she is debarred from the most profound insight into human nature by the respect which she pays to some unnatural convention'. This latter is not defined, and she goes on to say (wrongly, I believe) that Jane Austen uncritically accepts characters like Elinor and Fanny as good, 'without trying to see them in a fresh light for herself'.

Virginia Woolf is certainly at variance with Chesterton, seeing Jane Austen's art diminished by her failure to depict men. She felt that Jane Austen could not convey the 'power of the man', and the heroines are elevated in interest because the heroes 'are inferior to them in vitality and character'. In *Mansfield Park*, though, she breaks new ground, referring to the 'spirit and beauty of romance' in Fanny's rhapsody as she stands at the window with Edmund, and to the 'curious atmosphere of symbolism' in the scene where Maria and Henry Crawford 'refuse to wait for Rushworth, who is bringing the key of the gate'.

She regards Jane Austen's particular triumphs as being in her fools (who naturally include Mr Woodhouse and Miss Bates) – 'How various and individual is their folly'. She feels too that they are true to life in terms of the consistency of their foolishness, and that their other traits give them an overall verisimilitude. The memorable exchange between Mrs Bennet and Darcy in which she tells him that 'there is quite as much of that going on in the country as there is in town' leads her to think that the muddle and vacancy in Mrs Bennet's mind takes on a tragic dimension. It is a large claim.

Virginia Woolf holds that Jane Austen's satire lacks bitterness, believing that she seems to have been happy just observing people in their absurdity. It was 'Life itself' which absorbed her, and because of that, her novels are packed with it. Nothing is wasted, detail and observation are of the essence, and 'you cannot break off a scene or even a sentence without bleeding it of some of its life'. Wise and true words which define at one swoop the complexity and integrated completeness of the conception. Only those who write themselves can fully appreciate 'the wonder of her achievement, the imagination, the penetration, the insight' which she brought to bear on every incident she described. But Jane Austen's greatest gift is that she possessed 'the sense of the significance of life apart from any personal liking or disliking, of the beauty and continuity which underlies its trivial stream'. This is perceptive and lasting criticism, for although Virginia Woolf does not see what later critics have seen – Jane Austen's full absorption of her own background and the various ironic currents in their distinctive flow – she records enough to provide the basis for critical exploration which, I feel, has deepened as a result of her direct and independent appraisal.

Another major appraisal four years later came from Reginald Farrer in the *Quarterly Review* for July 1917, on the centenary of Jane Austen's death. As Southam observes, 'his essay remains one of the classic statements on Jane Austen'. He finds her securely established, well ahead of Miss Burney and Miss Edgeworth, to whom she was compared, though he admits that she has become 'the centre of a cult as ardent as a religion'. Farrer is occasionally misguided ('Women often appreciate her imperfectly, because she appreciated them so perfectly, and so inexorably revealed them'). He refers to Macaulay's comparison of Jane Austen with Shakespeare, observing that, 'both attain their solitary and special supremacy by dint of a common capacity for intense vitalisation', which means that they project 'not only a human being, but also something much greater than any one person, a quintessentialised instance of humanity, a generalisation made incarnate and personal by genius'. Both Shakespeare and Jane Austen exist only through their works, for from their lives we glean nothing 'but a little chopped chaff of details in which all trace of the sacred germ is lacking'. He hazards the guess, based on the idea that the novels do not give 'any

picture of united family happiness', that with regard to her
own family, 'She was in it; but she was not really of it'. There
is even the interesting assertion that 'after her first two
novels, she never again gives us a picture of two intimately
united sisters'.

Despite her own modest statements, she is not a limited
writer, and her personality may be profitably judged from her
work. But Farrer puts a high premium on impersonality:
'The self-revelation of the writer must be as severely implicit
as it is universally pervasive; it must never be conscious or
obtruded'. Only occasionally does she appear *in propria persona* (witness 'I quit such odious subjects' in *Mansfield Park*)
but generally eliminates herself in the interests of 'intense
concentration'. Farrer believes that first of all you convince
yourself 'in the game of make believe' and forget yourself by
concentrating 'with a single-eyed undeviating passion of
conviction, upon the tale you are setting out to live'. Everything else passes Jane Austen by: 'Her kingdoms are hermet-
ically sealed, in fact, and here lies the strength of their
impregnable immortality'. He maintains that she is never
'imprisoned' in any date and because of this she is never out
of date. In short, her truths are universal.

One of the reasons for her supremacy is 'a most perfect
mastery of her weapons, a most faultless and precise adjust-
ment of means to end'. Limitations of scene, he feels, do not
mean limitations of 'human emotion'. Again the universality
is stressed. She has the capacity to imply profound feeling,
as with the effect on Anne of her re-meeting Wentworth. She
is subtle and precise where others (like Henry James) are
wordy and woolly. She is 'even of an Elizabethan economy in
her stage-settings'. Her details are sparingly produced,
sometimes through conversational remarks. Farrer notes
the way she avails herself of the outer world in her later
novels, and in a fine phrase he says that 'Jane Austen has no
taste for expressed erotics'. Farrer covers her decision to omit
proposal scenes in her fictions, considering that this is evidence of her delicate discrimination, since such scenes are
difficult to express in words. Yet sometimes she is inconsistent, he feels, citing Fanny's rhetoric on two occasions in the

Vicarage shrubbery as evidence. Here Farrer is strong on reason and commendably blunt.

Most interesting is his conception of the nature of the woman behind the writing. Again, I suggest, he is ahead of his time, and indeed much more penetrating than many of those who followed him. He makes much of her iconoclastic tendencies, finding, as others have, a steely quality in her own penetration and a certain inflexibility in her judgement, particularly of moral issues. He believes that on the whole she feels that life is 'silly' and that she exposes, mercilessly, falseness and hypocrisy. Yet she is sympathetic to sincerity, is honest herself, takes no direct portraits from originals, but converts her own observations of people into positive identities of their own. Farrer asserts that 'Her very style is the accurate reflection of her nature'. She regards rational behaviour and standards as of the greatest importance, together with breeding which derives from a balanced contemplation of life. Farrer notes her scrupulous attention to detail in language, where a choice of word or nuance can convey vulgarity or affectation.

Farrer pleads for *Lady Susan* to be included in future editions of Jane Austen's work, since it provides evidence of her great strength and of her ability to develop a character particularity: he deduces that from the substance of *Lady Susan* there evolves ultimately the triumphs of Henry and Mary Crawford. Farrer is generally critical of *Sense and Sensibility*, but praises *Pride and Prejudice* for its dextrous achievements which, he feels, she never tried to repeat later. At the same time, he feels that Jane Austen left herself open to the kind of misinterpretation of which Scott was guilty, namely that Elizabeth was moved to revise her (supposed) attitude towards Darcy once she had seen Pemberley.

Farrer believes that Jane Austen should be read deliberately, carefully and never quickly. He notes her sheer delight in creating such characters as Lady Catherine de Bourgh and Mr Collins, something I suspect we share. But even Farrer is prone to odd inverted judgements, finding that *Northanger Abbey* 'takes a big stride forward' since in it Jane Austen has successfully combined the elements of parody with major dramatic concerns. His argument is a cunning one – for he establishes in his own judgement that there is a unifying emphasis which consists of an artful echoing or mingling of comic art and intense feeling.

At this stage Farrer switches (unproductively I feel) to Jane Austen's move to Bath, but when he comes to the final sequence of her writing he suggests that 'laughter' is absent from her late novels. His consideration of *Mansfield Park* is neatly balanced between extreme praise and a sense of limitations. He praises the 'technical mastery' and the realism of the conception, but finds the novel 'is vitiated throughout by a radical dishonesty'. It is an unfortunate and indefensible remark. Farrer obviously feels that Jane Austen is split between 'clerical' edification (the biography of Edmund Bertram) and what he calls 'unprompted joy in creation'. Nothing could be farther from the truth. There is no split motive or conception, and although the weakness of Tom Bertram's repentance is rightly stigmatized, it is erroneous to criticize Jane Austen for what is here defined as the conflict between her moral appraisal of the Crawfords and her affection for them as creations. There is no incompatibility: it is rather that the critic has failed to appreciate the shifting perspective of the Austen irony. Similarly, Farrer suggests that the elopement of Henry Crawford and Maria is a 'flagrant fraud' (this is not an unusual emphasis). Again we feel the limitation of the appraisal: the preparations for the elopement are to be found within the text; it grows naturally out of the earlier sequences and the characters' frailty.

Farrer continues in full rhetorical flow, saving some of his strongest critical invective for the presentation and effect of Fanny Price, whom he considers a 'female prig-pharisee'. Her sense of self-righteousness is impregnable, and he finds her guilty of inflexible prejudice. After this we might expect praise for Mary Crawford, and we get it in the subjectively cloying assertion that she would have made a delightful and intelligent wife. She is, Farrer feels, 'the most persistently brilliant of Jane Austen's heroines'. But this is qualified in a sense by his assertion that *Emma* is on all counts a much

greater novel. He emphasizes the complexity of the structure, the total relevance and the artistic control. He feels that
the author reaches new heights in her presentation of character – *Emma* is superlatively a novel of character – and he
is particularly incisive and original in his examination of
Emma herself. Many readers, he argues, are put off by
Emma, but he insists that Jane Austen's triumph is to solve
the problem of her heroine, and to demonstrate through her
ironic modes that we should not be guilty of taking that
heroine seriously. It is an ingenious theory, based on his idea
that Emma 'is simply a figure of fun', but extended to embrace the fact that this is high comedy indeed, that the reader
retains affection for the character despite the faults that
character possesses, or even because of them. In fact, he
describes our reactions to Emma as 'poised'; they are capable
of movement in each direction, from laughter to disapproval
and vice-versa. This leads him to a contemplation of other
characters in this novel, finding that they too provoke our
disapproval as well as our smiles. There is also a note on Jane
Fairfax, who had to be made 'dim' so that she would not be
brought into competition with the brilliant (and brilliantly
misguided) Emma.

By comparison, *Persuasion* is 'fitful' and 'wayward'. It is
uneven, with soft and hard irregularities, and there is a
failure in the ending – 'the whole Clay-Elliot embroglio that
cuts the non-existent knot at the end of the book is perhaps
the clumsiest of Jane Austen's *coups de theâtre*, though not
as deliberately false as that of *Mansfield Park*'. He balances
this by praising the conception of Anne Elliot – 'one of fiction's
greatest heroines'. He feels that *Persuasion* is 'a cry of feeling', and that here Jane Austen has 'reached the culminating
point in her art of conveying emotion without expression'
(Farrer means without an overt flood of emotion: reticence is
an implication of deep feeling). He draws a comparison with
Marianne, saying that 'there is more intensity of emotion in
Anne's calm'.

Farrer makes a positive contribution to Jane Austen criticism. Bearing in mind the period in which he is writing, he
displays a commendable attention to detail in the texts and

a detailed knowledge of them. His main weakness is a tendency to subjectivity and an occasional misreading, but the level of criticism and the identification of subtlety and high art are impressive. Farrer is one of those whose maturity of appraisal and suggestions of depth in Jane Austen paved the way for so much 20th-century investigation.

E.M. Forster considered himself a 'Jane Austenite' as distinct, I suppose, from a Janeite, and although there is a deal of self-mockery in his pose, his praise of the Chapman edition of the novels in 1924 shows the depth of his sympathetic affiliations. He is considering what we now call annotation and commentary: 'The novels continue to live their own wonderful internal life, but it has been freshened and enriched by contact with the life of facts'. Chapman's background density is indeed impressive, 'and even his textual criticism helps'. By recognising Chapman's contribution, his keen eye and his checking which leads to a virtually definitive text, Forster puts an important seal of approval on the literary scholarship to come in our own time. He picks out the example in *Pride and Prejudice* where one of Mr Bennet's lines had hitherto been given to Kitty: Chapman apportions it correctly, with the result that 'The dialogue lights up and sends a little spark of fire into the main mass of the novel'. A similar detail of emendation is cited in *Mansfield Park*, another more important example picked up through collation of editions in *Sense and Sensibility*.

Virginia Woolf also reviewed the Oxford edition in 'Jane Austen at Sixty' (*Athenaeum*, 15 December 1923), but her emphasis is speculative rather than scholarly. She takes a close look at *Persuasion* and notes Jane Austen's asperity in her treatment of Sir Walter and his eldest daughter. But she feels that in *Persuasion* Jane Austen is 'beginning to discover that the world is larger, more mysterious, and more romantic than she had supposed'. There is a deliberately invoked autumnal sadness about *Persuasion*. Virginia Woolf feels that Jane Austen's 'attitude to life itself is altered', that this is conditioned by her own unhappiness, and 'Therefore the observation is less of facts and more of feelings than is usual'. But the speculation about what would have happened – she would have lived in London had she lived, runs the theme, and taken a store of observations 'to feast upon at leisure' – is, of course, beyond our or any other critical belief. One point is that there would have been less dialogue and more observation, judging from the evidence of *Persuasion*, while comments such as 'She would have been the forerunner of Henry James and of Proust' are redundant. Virginia Woolf admits that her speculations are vain, but I touch upon them here because they are indications of the deepening interest in Jane Austen and a concern to record and evaluate everything about her and her works: Virginia Woolf is bringing to bear not only her intellect but her imagination, positive signs of the enduring appeal which Jane Austen was beginning to exert.

In 1925 Edith Wharton could say (in *The Writing of Fiction*) that *Emma* is an outstanding instance of 'a novel in which character shapes events quietly but irresistibly, as a stream nibbles away its banks'. Three years later Arnold Bennett wrote in the *Evening Standard* that Jane Austen inspired such fanatical worship that he feared to denigrate her, though his own admiration for her had been increased by repeated readings. He then places her not among the great but the 'great little' novelists, because her world is 'tiny' and she omits so much. She 'has never been beaten in the field of pure comedy' and 'She loved her social system – but had no (or few) illusions about it'. For Bennett, small may be beautiful, but it is not universal, and he reflects the limitations of perspective which bedevil so much early Austen criticism.

In 1932 Rebecca West noted two important aspects of Jane Austen's art. Her commentary is in the preface to *Northanger Abbey* and the first publisher's cavalier treatment of the manuscript. Miss West considers its 'novelty' and feels that this is why the publisher neglected it for so long. But she notes what was later to be explored in depth: as she puts it, Jane Austen was almost certainly 'indirectly influenced by the sceptical movement of the eighteenth century which came to a climax in the French Revolution'. Next, she stresses the 'feminism' of Jane Austen, referring to the attack on the *Spectator* and the 'slighting references to women common in

that work' in *Northanger Abbey*. Jane Austen's identification
with Catherine Morland establishes this – like Jane, she is
'one of a country parson's brood'. She goes on: 'Everywhere it
was pretended that women were heroines...and that in any
case it was distinterested desire which dictated the relationship of the sexes'. Jane Austen shows the truth by puncturing
these illusions through her portrait of General Tilney, but
'wealth of the mind counts in the female sex as a kind of
poverty'. The idea of romantic love is shattered, and women
like Isabella Thorpe have to employ 'counter-calculation'.
Miss West notes that prior to Jane Austen coquettes were
drawn by men, whereas Isabella realized that 'there was no
way of independence and the pleasantest way of dependence
was matrimony'. The position of women is more important
in *Northanger Abbey* than the satire on Gothic novels, while
the outstanding qualities of the novel itself are indicated: 'It
is sharp with Jane Austen's hate of unpleasant things, it is
sweet with her love of all that is pleasant, it nourishes with
her special wit that is the extremity of good sense; and her
genius for character-drawing is at its happiest here'. This is
fine, balanced criticism: Miss West says in brief compass
what much 20th-century probing has said, more fully, but
with less sense of perspective.

H.W. Garrod's 'Depreciation' (1928, read to the Royal Society of Literature) need not be taken too seriously, since it
is a reaction against Janeitism. It stigmatizes superficiality,
narrowness and complacency, and is animated by an extreme
subjectivity, a resentment of the Jane Austen cult. But it
lacks coherence and sustained investigation: a welter of
prejudices are rhetoricized with more than a little pride, and
one gets the feeling that the judgements derive not from close
re-reading but from closer self-absorption. Garrod's squib
has been put out by the many jets of sharply directed analysis
which have elevated Jane Austen on the undeniable merits
of her art.

4

Mid-20th-Century Biography and Criticism

There are few more important studies of Jane Austen than that of Mary Lascelles' *Jane Austen and Her Art* (1939). It is both scholarly and imaginative, selecting and interpreting, based on width and depth of reading in the period, and expressed in exemplary manner. The first section is devoted to biography, and she takes issue with those who say that Jane Austen herself was disagreeable – 'it is based on one coarse and ill-natured passage, two or three ill-humoured and two or three sharply satirical passages, in her letters'. Miss Lascelles' biographical treatment is succinct and measured: it is typical of the living quality of her association that she wishes, if any more letters came to light, they would be 'Cassandra's rather than Jane to Cassandra'. There is an admirable critical summary of *Volume the First, Volume the Second and Volume the Third*: she indicates the easy transition from *Lesley Castle* and *The Three Sisters* to *Elinor and Marianne*, and traces the development of the latter into *Sense and Sensibility*. The revisions of this novel are considered in relation to particular references – for example, to biographies of Cowper and to Scott's *Marmion*.

Miss Lascelles has a generosity of spirit when it comes to acknowledging others. She cites K. Metcalfe's introduction to *Pride and Prejudice* in 1912, where he wrote of Jane Austen and her art: 'A rational woman, exceptional in intellect, unique in wit, found herself in circumstances which were always meagre, and times irrational; and endowed with fastidiousness on the one hand and enjoyment on the other, she employed her experience creatively in the service of Comedy'. Miss Lascelles believes that a new period of life and creative activity began for Jane Austen after the Bath experience when she went to Chawton in 1809. The focus is sharp. She notes Jane's capacity – she was working on *Pride and Prejudice* and *Mansfield Park* at the same time as she was correcting the proofs of *Sense and Sensibility* – 'as an achievement which shows that she could project her imagination into one or another of these fragile bubble worlds and let it dwell there'. Jane Austen began *Mansfield Park* diffidently, but grew in confidence – 'She must have known that *Mansfield Park* excelled *Pride and Prejudice* in its subtler conception of human relations'. Miss Lascelles' saturation in her subject is reflected in her comments on the minor works: she observes of *Sanditon* that 'it is a hilarious comedy of invalidism, and (what was even less to be expected) a bold venture in a new way of telling a story'. Always she is aware of Jane Austen's progress, of her responses to her reading as she 'tries to formulate and solve the problems of her art'.

Miss Lascelles' discussion of reading and response (her title) evaluates both Jane Austen's style and the 'management of her narrative material'. She notes the influence of Johnson (as moral writer) and of Cowper, and observes that 'allusions to books run like an undercurrent' through Jane Austen's works. With her, selection and emphases are important. Her contemporaries often over-quoted (so does a character like Mrs Elton), and she traces the development of burlesque control from the early works through to the mature novels where they become 'an integral part of the narrative'. She notes the connection between *The Orphan of the Castle* (1788) and *Northanger Abbey*, where the burlesque 'has a pretty intimacy and variety', while in *Sense and Sensibility* 'it is subtle'. Miss Lascelles is strong too on the incidence of illusion and illusory worlds in the fiction, saying of *Emma* that it 'presents a deliberately contrived antithesis between the worlds of actuality and illusion'. This is a neat

summary of Jane Austen's subtle structural art. Miss Lascelles also analyses the way the catastrophes are handled in
each of the novels, recording the humour which derives from
Louisa's fall in *Persuasion*, where the labourers on the Cobb
have the apparent sight of 'two dead young ladies'. This
emphasis 'pricks in an instant the bubble catastrophe'.

The investigation of style ('Proper words in proper places'
is Johnson's illustration from Swift) registers Jane Austen's
dislike of elaborate sentence structures 'that go against the
grain of language', and the observation that 'her *hollow*
people have a taste for double negatives' – witness General
Tilney and Mr Collins. Miss Lascelles notes the development
of her style, and how she succeeded in making herself mistress of a variety of tones. Her own 'playfulness and epigram-
maticism...exactly hits off the narrative manner of *Pride and
Prejudice*'. Dialogue is Jane Austen's particular strength: she
has 'a precocious quickness of ear' and is an alert observer of
mannerisms in speech. Miss Lascelles' tone so often complements that of her subject: she refers to the *'limpid confusion'*
of Miss Bates' talk and to Jane Austen's mastery of syntax
and phrasing as the modes of differentiation. Her style is
pliable, having a 'curiously chameleon-like faculty'. She has
a wonderful delight in absurdity which 'vibrates' in her
characters' conversation, and there is the incidence of 'anti-
thetic phrasing' which perhaps derives again from Dr
Johnson. She is 'shy of figurative language' and rejects 'novel
slang'.

Miss Lascelles quotes Katherine Mansfield's defence of
Jane Austen against her detractors who 'said she was not a
lady, was not fond of children, hated animals, did not care a
pin for the poor, could not have written about foreign parts
if she had tried, had no idea about how a fox was killed... –
was, in short, cold, coarse, practically illiterate and without
morality'. Her reply to this may have been, 'Ah, but what
about my novels?'. Miss Lascelles goes on to stress Jane
Austen's 'constant tranquil preference for a true over a false
vision of life'. She notices her power of exclusion, for example,
of death, but the sense of individual and overall perspective
is strikingly integrated and admirably consistent: 'all Jane

Austen's characters, the fools with the rest, have the mental
qualities proper to them, to their wisdom or to their
folly...and if I wanted to know what happened in Highbury
on any particular day I should go to Miss Bates – just as, if I
wanted counsel, I would rather ask it of Bottom than of
anyone else in Athens'. This is an endorsement of Macaulay's
analogy through imaginative association.

This study indicates occasional weaknesses as well as
incontrovertible strengths: Miss Lascelles feels that Darcy
volunteers too much information in his letter to Elizabeth for
'a proud and reserved man – unless under pressure from his
author, anxious to get on with the story'. But she emphasizes
the 'practice of forethought' and the 'Factual verisimilitude'
(casually undermined in *Emma* by mentioning an orchard in
blossom at midsummer). There is the important development in Jane Austen's art 'of the technique of self-efface-
ment', the importance of the sense of place in her works,
though it is not 'concrete particularisation', and the fine use
of contrasts, as in Mansfield-Portsmouth in *Mansfield Park*.
Miss Lascelles returns to *Sanditon*, endorsing E.M. Forster's
'Topography comes to the front' by saying that 'Sanditon is
certainly a force, an agent, perhaps even one might say a
character in the story'. She believes however that 'treatment
of *place* is best studied in *Persuasion*'.

Linked to this sense of place is a complementary sense of
time. Changes of pace are discussed, and she records Jane
Austen's ability 'to give some impression of double time by
contrasting the beat (as it were) of Elinor's normal with
Marianne's feverish pulse'. In *Mansfield Park* Jane Austen
uses the ' "calendar-time" of the world as we know it and
"personal time" of human beings as we know them'. Other
particularities in Jane Austen's art include her ability to
present the consciousness of her characters, her convincing
definition of servants, and the establishing of a perspective
between author and reader. Point of view in character as a
reflection of the author's own standpoint is evaluated, as well
as the modes of irony which Jane Austen employs. There is
consistency overall, but flexibility within this. She notes that
Jane Austen has 'a parental interest in the beings she

created' according to the *Memoir* and our own feelings, instancing 'a tenderness as towards a child' in the conception of Fanny Price. Miss Lascelles' final words are, for this reader at least, definitive of Jane Austen's effect and achievement. She writes of her 'close and genial relationship with the familiar, daylight world...a scrupulous fidelity to the evidence at her disposal; mastery, moreover, of her chosen methods of representation, wise use of all the resources she can command, of her own powers and her reader's capacity for response'. The emphases here reflect the scrupulous dedication of their author.

D.W. Harding began his investigation of Jane Austen in *Scrutiny* in 1940; it is probably true to say that he exerted a profound influence of disagreement and a measure of sympathetic affinity. The Jane Austen of popular impression and in some instances adoration would not have attracted him as a reader in the first instance. 'Regulated Hatred' describes what he discovered for himself (which was against the common view), that 'her scope was of course extemely restricted, but that within her limits she succeeded admirably in expressing the gentler virtues of a civilised social order'. She was thought of as a 'delicate satirist', with her 'inevitable lightness of touch' revealing 'the comic foibles and amiable weaknesses of the people whom she lived amongst and liked'. Harding asserts that the 'total effect is false'. In *Emma* she 'invites her readers to be just their natural patronising selves'. He selects Miss Bates, and by close attention to detail here suggests that Jane Austen brought 'fear and hatred into the relationships of everyday social life', and that her dialogue and innuendoes change 'the flavour of the more ordinary satire amongst which it is embedded'.

Another centre of focus is on the Coles' dinner party. Here, Harding says that she is not guilty of 'didactic intention'. He feels that there is a distinct motivation behind her writing, and finds that she uses it in order to embody her own critical attitudes. In *Emma* she breaks new ground by relegating the 'Cinderella theme' to a secondary role, thus re-examining the relationship of her heroine to others. He regards this as 'bold', showing that she was capable of change and development, and that she was re-thinking her own attitude towards her own structures.

Other interesting emphases in support of his thesis are his notation of Henry Tilney's reprimand to Catherine Morland for her Gothic suspicions of his father: Harding cunningly omits from his quotation the loaded clause which underlines that there is no way of concealment in English society, 'where every man is surrounded by a neighbourhood of voluntary spies'. He also asserts that one of her most telling and revealing modes is to deliberately present as caricatures – 'exaggerated figures of fun' – types of people whom she dislikes and is perhaps afraid of, such as Mrs Bennet. He feels that caricature suited Jane Austen's purpose, and shows the double dimensions of her particular scenes. He observes (of Mr Collins' brief courtship of Elizabeth) that the proposal has elements of 'comic fantasy', but also for Elizabeth a nightmareish quality because of her vulnerable situation – she is, if you like, subject to the market forces of marriage and of her father's failure to provide for his family. It is because of this situation that the two dimensions are evident: for Elizabeth 'the comic monster' is too close for comfort, too near success merely to be dismissed by laughter. We do not have to agree with Harding, but we cannot fail to be stimulated by the incisive and sustained directness of his commentary. He is not presenting a new Jane Austen, but allowing the hitherto unnoticed or submerged part of her literary personality to surface. The result is positive criticism, a gain in dimensional perception of what she achieves. He finds 'priggishness' in *Mansfield Park*, and I suspect that many of us would agree, though modern critics have tended to cut past it through elaborate analysis and explanation. Harding probes, finding that the reason for his conclusion derives from 'the curiously abortive attempt at humility' which is to be found in the novel. There is much truth in this and Harding, perhaps unconsciously, was charting new areas for Jane Austen criticism. The results have been clearly seen since he wrote this fifty years ago. Perhaps it can be summarized by saying that there has been distinct progression from assumptions of delicacy and slightness (or even 'charm') to a major, greater indication of the fullness of the literary personality indicated above. When read today, Harding's comments have a freshness of utterance and a concentrated vigour which challenges our own assumptions and the quality of our reading, giving us pause for re-thinking and re-evaluating what we had come to accept.

In *Jane Austen: Facts and Problems* (1948) R.W. Chapman provides a complementary volume to the letters and works, some of it reproducing 'facts' or 'problems' from the former. Much time is spent on tracing the family and then indicating its strength and spread: 'Six sons and two daughters were born at Steventon, all of whom survived their father. Five of the sons had nine wives and had issue'. There is little wonder that he can describe the canvas of Jane Austen's life as being crowded with 'sisters-in-law, nephews and nieces'. But the numerate emphasis is replaced by family appraisal, brief and telling, for example, on Cassandra, where he says that she was of regular habits and settled opinions, family legend crediting her with being superior to Jane. Chapman traces the sisters' schooling, at the Abbey school in Reading in Jane's case, spicing the account with his own opinions – that Jane Austen owed much to books but more to observation, and that 'English society as Jane Austen depicts it shows a sharp cleavage between the nobility and the gentry'. He notes the influence of her cousin Eliza on her, particularly through the theatrical rehearsals, and engages with H.W. Garrod's famous assertion of Jane Austen that 'It would be difficult to name a writer of similar eminence who possessed so little knowledge of literature' by indicating the amount of reading revealed in the letters. Many of these he finds so entertaining that they 'can hardly be read aloud with gravity'. The traumas of the Bath period are spelled out, and Chapman writes of the Steventon time that 'Jane's local attachments were of extraordinary strength; they were no small part of her genius'. There are some pertinent comments on the unique mode of *Lady Susan*, the inevitable biographical speculation about Tom Lefroy ('At length the day is come on which I am to flirt my last with Tom Lefroy'), and other romantic emphases. After dating the revisions and works of the Chawton period, Chapman proceeds to discuss Jane Austen's character and opinions. He cites Harold Nicholson's verdict on Jane Austen's 'appalling gentility of style and aspect' and that she had a mind 'like a very small, sharp pair of scissors' and contrasts these with her brother Henry's conclusion in the *Biographical Notice* of 1817 that 'her opinions accorded strictly with those of our Established Church'. As Chapman observes slyly, 'in 1817 there was no bathos in concluding a character with a certificate of orthodoxy'. Chapman's own conclusions are often modest – 'Her books, with all their variety of excellence, are unpretentious love-stories' – a statement which would hardly account for her pre-eminence in the world of English letters.

Interestingly, his emphases embrace the emotional areas so often neglected in any appraisal of Jane Austen: 'The secret of enduring fiction is sympathy and passion – an emotional not an intellectual endowment', and this is extended by crediting Jane Austen with 'largeness of soul'. Thus, she ensures that her sympathy includes 'the objects of her ridicule', though she keeps to her own imposed structures, hardly ever allowing herself 'a male conversation without female audience' in her fiction. She is aware of the decorum imposed upon lady novelists: 'In the first edition of *Sense and Sensibility* Mrs Jennings does mention a natural son; but this was expunged in the second'. There is a considered appraisal of her accuracy of hedgerow description and chronology (witness her Bath episodes), which leads one to think 'that her creative imagination worked most freely within a framework fixed for her by small points of contact with reality'. Chapman covers the sequence of her anonymity, then what he exaggerates by calling her notoriety. There is a very useful section on biography and criticism, though we may take issue with the claim that the Austen-Leighs' work (1913) 'may fairly be called a definitive life'.

Chapman returns to Bradley's essay of 1911, in which he asserted that 'The subject of her art is not individuals, but their interaction'. Chapman notes Walter Raleigh's recognition (in *The English Novel*, p. 263) that 'the world of pathos and passion is present in her work by implication'. Chapman himself believes that 'Her satire is merciless; it admits no extenuation, but it is not misanthropy'. In praising Jane Austen's works he quotes what Boswell derived from Johnson – 'Bark and steel for the mind'.

Chapman's final sections are, in effect, a review with bibliographical tastings up to 1948. Writing about when Jane Austen called the publisher John Murray a rogue and herself a mercenary author, he observes 'These denunciations will not be taken very seriously except by those critics who choose to believe her sincere when she confesses a vice, and hypocritical when she assumes a virtue'. Many of his references are covered elsewhere in this study, but he fills in details with meticulous responsibility, saying of *Brabourne* (1884) that he gives 'a full account of Jane Austen's life in Kent, of which the *Memoir* knows little'. E.M. Forster's evaluation of *Sanditon*, in which he found signs of fatigue but also 'a change of tone which might have led her to a new criticism of life' is set against his depreciation of the letters. Virginia Woolf's superb focus (included in *The Common Reader*, 1925) registers Jane Austen's 'exquisite discrimination of human values' and observes that 'of all great writers [she is the] most difficult to catch in the act of greatness'. Chapman also selects the most significant for-and-against statements, condemning H.W. Garrod's 'Jane Austen: a Depreciation' by saying 'His sophistry is weighted and sharpened by a genuine distaste for his subject', an underlining of Garrod's own comment on his essay – 'the malice is the best part of it'. There is much praise for Lord David Cecil's Leslie Stephen Lecture (Cambridge 1935), which Chapman considers 'the only brief account of Jane Austen as an artist and a moralist that is completely satisfactory'. Mary Lascelles (see pp. 43-7) is 'perhaps a critic's critic, and moves in a rare atmosphere'. This is, one feels, an indication of Chapman's own limitations. He does, however, cite two of Cecil's more stimulating statements: the first is on what might be called Jane Austen's moral economy – 'It was wrong to marry for money, but it was silly to marry without it', while the second asserts that in going off with Maria, Henry Crawford was behaving 'in a manner wholly inconsistent with the rest of his character'.

Chapman has his own favourites, joining with Forster to praise the particular excellences and newness of *Sanditon*. *Emma* is pre-eminent though. It is 'among other things a detective story', and it has a 'matchless symmetry of design', an 'endless fascination' of technique, but above all there is 'the flow of blood beneath the smooth polished skin'. Chapman's industry, his sympathetic association with the Jane Austen ethos and his summaries of what was written about her, are an invaluable contribution to the historical appraisal of her work. He lacks critical sophistication but compensates for this by his dedication.

Among other books Chapman cites Elizabeth Jenkins' *Jane Austen: A Biography* (1938) which he calls 'a singularly honest book, the spontaneous effusion of real affection'. It is an appropriate emphasis. Miss Jenkins never allows her saturation in Jane Austen and her times to weigh down her own narrative flair: 'At sixteen Jane Austen could choose at random a handful of people, to whom no extraneous interest whatever attached itself, either of beauty, character or circumstance, and breathe such life into them that while we are occupied with them we are not conscious of what they are without'. Miss Jenkins' style is relaxed and attractive, but the failure to record sources through some form of reference means that we feel (often, I suggest) that we are reading a biography which is clothed in the form of a novel. Nothing must be allowed to impede the narrative flow: the Jane Austen story, like Jane Austen's stories, is dramatically done, as with the arrival of Willoughby at the end of a chapter. Twentieth-century analogies with Jane Austen's period are sprinkled throughout the text. But the tone of the study is warm with sympathy and appreciation, and there is evidence throughout of a scrupulous attention to period detail.

Jane Austen's preoccupation with dress, at least in her letters, is noted, and there is a detailed account of her life at Bath and of the Leigh Perrot theft case: interesting though this is (it is a must for biographers) there is perhaps too much space accorded to it. Speculation about Jane Austen's love affairs is moderately handled, marred only by an indulgent and subjective account of how she feels Jane would have reacted to adversity ('She was not the woman to be prostrated by a love affair' or to withdraw 'till the beauty of the world became a torment instead of a consolation'). Can we know? There is some intelligent evaluation of *Northanger Abbey*, and a particular emphasis on *The Watsons* which seems to this reader at least to show Miss Jenkins at her best – as critic rather than biographer. She observes that 'there is something painful in *The Watsons*. It is a study, of uncompromising realism, of three women desperately anxious to get themselves married', and it is done, Miss Jenkins feels, with 'a realism as sordid as Flaubert's'.

After further discriminating analysis of *Lady Susan* and a biographical tracing of the move to Southampton, Miss Jenkins expresses the view (despite the presentation of the Middleton children in *Sense and Sensibility*) that Jane Austen loved children, a view she derives from the letters. These (and Chapman) are greatly praised: they are 'a treasury of interest and delight' and also 'an expression, as it were, of the raw material, unsifted and unrefined, out of which the novels were composed'. With this we must agree, and there is a refreshing and direct commentary on the earthiness which some of these letters display. The detail on the Chawton period is given (according to Edward's remark, Jane Austen had now given up being fashionable), which shows her still deft at sewing and dextrous at games 'such as spillikins or cup and ball'. As always, Miss Jenkins' critical comments are incisive: she says that when re-reading *Pride and Prejudice* she had a marked sense of surprise at its compactness. But she feels that there is 'steel' within it, and that Darcy's character exists 'independent of circumstances', a sure underlining of Jane Austen's sense, intuitive and reasoned, of psychological integration. The letters form the essential background to the evaluation of the novels, but Miss Jenkins sometimes draws analogies which strike the reader by their essential truth, as when she compares *Pride and Prejudice* and *Mansfield Park*, in their effects, to *L'Allegro* and *Il Penseroso*. There is an intelligent appreciation of *Lover's Vows*, and again a sharp focus on Eaton Stannard Barrett's skit on Mrs Radcliffe called *The Heroine*, which Jane Austen loved.

Some of her independent assertions are questionable, for example, as when she notes that in *Emma* Jane Austen dwells much on class divisions. This fails, I think, to recognize the informed directions of the ironic mode; it may be disagreeable to the unenlightened, but its accuracy is surely unquestionable. Miss Jenkins notes, as others have done, Jane Austen's advice on writing fiction to her niece Anna. Its essence is of course the much-quoted expression of deliberate, self-imposed confinement – 'three or four families in a country village is the very thing to work on'. With the recognition of her work by the Prince Regent, Jane Austen, as if aware of her public persona as distinct from the shared family secret, collects a list of comments comprising a small anthology of criticism on *Emma*.

Miss Jenkins proceeds to some generalizations about the novels. Her book is much more than a popular biography: it also makes astute critical and social comments of a stimulating nature. She identifies one of the enduring qualities of Jane Austen's appeal, and that is the explicit and direct language which she uses. It presents no difficulty, and is the result of her detailed attention to her art in making 'a style composed of those elements of language which do not date'.

5

The Letters

R.W. Chapman's edition of the *Letters* (2nd edition, 1952) contains a forthright and definitive introduction, although the letters themselves did much to diminish Jane Austen's popularity. Unlike some of the correspondence of great writers, these show little evidence of having been written for posterity. Chapman reveals his independent judgement in his introduction and, although there are errors, his attention to family detail and identifications adds much to the bare contemplation of the texts. He says that it is his impression 'that Cassandra Austen was not the correspondent who best evoked her sister's powers', which reads like an advance apology for dullness. He follows this with the assertion that Jane Austen's own letters are memorable: 'Read with attention, they yield a picture of the life of the upper middle class of that time which is surely without a rival. And they depict not only manners, but also persons', a statement later expanded into 'And though the characterisation is incidental, and hardly ever deliberate, it is by the same hand as Lady Bertram and Mrs Norris [even if] the *Letters* are, like most letters, occasional, unstudied, and inconsequent...they straggle...they straggle over twenty years, and lack a plot'. This is true, but Chapman insists that the range of the letters more than compensates for this.

His tone is tolerant, and he says that the letters often possess 'gentle or playful malice' though it is unfair to conclude that Miss Austen was deficient in the softer emotions,

just as it is unfair to deny her all romantic sentiment because
there, too, she knew her limitations, and declared she 'could
no more write a romance than an epic poem'. In fact, there is
evidence in the early letters that she was able to produce
burlesque romance in her own case. She writes that she
expects 'to receive an offer from my friend in the course of
the evening. I shall refuse him, however, unless he promises
to give away his white coat' (14 January 1796). She also has
a capacity for self-mockery, for example, as seen in 'At length
the day is come on which I am to flirt my last with Tom Lefroy,
and when you receive this it will be over. My tears flow as I
write at the melancholy idea' (ibid.). The play of her humour
is delightful, as she takes pleasure in affecting to preserve a
secret which everybody knows about, when she writes asking
to be remembered to everybody who failed to ask after her,
or as in 'Miss Fletcher and I were very thick, but I am the
thinnest of the two'. She even mocks her own attendance on
her mother during the latter's illness as being 'very grand'
and self-important. There is also of course the celebrated
remark about the woman whose child was born dead because
she was frightened by something (Jane suggests her husband
[27 October 1798]). Again one feels that the *tone* of this has
been misjudged, and that there is more reflex irony than
malice in it.

Outward physical appraisal is accorded a like emphasis.
'Mrs Portman is not much admired in Dorsetshire; the good-
natured world, as usual, extolled her beauty so highly, that
all the neighbourhood have had the pleasure of being disap-
pointed' (17 November 1798). The self-laughter extends to
her own dress and appearance, as in (after she has altered a
cap) 'I think it makes me look more like Lady Conyngham
than it did before, which is all that one lives for now' (18
December 1798). At this time in her life she seems to have
had a great interest in attending balls (and sometimes a
cynical appraisal of them), and in her naval brothers' assign-
ments and promotions. The interest in clothes is always
present, and there is a note of her charities to the poor. There
is an early mention of *First Impressions*, the original title of
Pride and Prejudice (she says that Martha is quite capable

of publishing it 'from memory, and one more perusal must enable her to do it'). Such incidents as the destruction of trees in high winds are recorded, but it is her public interactions – her responses to visitors, for example – which are seen in a snippet such as 'I was as civil to them as their bad breath would allow me' (20 November 1800). The mockery of romantic expectations is reflected in 'Why did you dance four dances with so stupid a Man?', when the alternative was to dance with one of his fellow officers who might have responded to her attractions by falling in love (14 January 1801).

Jane Austen records the sale of her books and pianoforte when they move to Bath, and there gives her impressions of an 'Adultress' who seemed 'rather quietly and contentedly silly than anything else' (12 May 1801). There are two moving letters to her brother Frank on their father's death (21 and 22 January 1805). Later, the changed circumstances, the reduction of their living standards and the adjusted social situation, are keenly evidenced. Literary judgements of her contemporaries are occasionally present – there is the condemnation of *Clarentine* for its triviality (8 February 1807) and 'ought I to be very much pleased with *Marmion*? – as yet I am not' (20 June 1808). Her own wisdom about herself and others – something which is characteristic of her own writing – is often found, for example, in 'Nobody ever feels or acts, suffers or enjoys, as one expects' (30 June 1808). Jane Austen's letters are not as slight or as trivial in substance as some of her more trenchant critics have said. They are trivial in the sense that human nature has a reflex triviality which often mixes the wise and the sensitive with the superficial and the irritating. Jane Austen, in fact, runs the gamut of response, here the cloyingly conventional, as when she writes of her sister-in-law Elizabeth's death – 'We need not enter into a Panegyric on the Departed – but it is sweet to think of her great worth, of her solid principles, her true devotion, her excellence in every relation of life' (13 October 1808). I do not detect irony here, but rather the need to be saying the right things and the assurance that Cassandra will think them fitting. This also applies to her response to a wedding – 'Dr Phillot to Lady Frances St Lawrence. *She* wanted to have a

husband, I suppose, once in her life, and *he* a Lady Frances'
(24 October 1808).

Much excitement is generated by the removal to Chawton,
though even this is coloured with irony – 'Mrs H. Digweed
looks forward with great satisfaction to our being her neighbours. I would have her enjoy the idea to the utmost, as I
suspect there will not be much in the reality' (27 December
1808). She writes in octosyllabic couplets to her brother
Frank, congratulating him on the birth of a boy (26 July
1809), though the lines also include some bathos on Chawton
('And how convinced, that when complete/ It will all other
houses beat'). Writing and gardening absorb her attention at
this time, she reads a book on the British Empire, and
exclaims with parental fondness about having her 'darling
child' when *Pride and Prejudice* arrives (29 January 1813).
Her possessiveness, pride and prejudice are shown in this
letter, but as so often they are inlaid with a self-mocking
humour, as when she speaks with exaggerated praise of her
heroine as being one of the most 'delightful' ever created, and
of her own intolerance of anyone who should dare to criticize
her. She goes on to say how she had cut the novel, but now
feels that it might have been stretched out by the use of
contrasting matter, at the same time coyly describing her
own style as being full of 'playfulness and epigrammatism'
(4 February 1813).

From now on, the main interest in her letters is to be found
in the comments she makes on her own writing, the jokes she
has about her own characters as portraits in exhibitions, and
the confession that she has something with which to follow
Pride and Prejudice (though she does not believe that it will
provide nearly as much entertainment [3 July 1813]). She
visits London and attends the theatre (September 1813) with
some disappointment, and her observation of society both
here and at home becomes increasingly barbed. There is
much delightful and self-mocking humour about her own
appearance as she gets older, as when she is thought by one
of her acquaintances to be much 'handsomer than she expected' (6 November 1813). She repeats her brother Henry's
reactions to *Mansfield Park* in which he expressed his liking

for the art which produced Lady Bertram and Mrs Norris. She confidently assumes that he understood all the characters and that he could see how everything would be resolved (2 March 1814). Later, he expressed his admiration for Henry Crawford. Meanwhile, she continues to visit the theatre, seeing Kean at Drury Lane and saying that she has had enough of Covent Garden for the time being.

Of much interest about this time is her friendly criticism and advice to her niece Anna, whose novel she is reading. Jane Austen pays particular attention, as we might expect, to propriety and structure. Her comments are forthright, and she feels that Anna's descriptions of place are too detailed and that they will not be appreciated (9 September 1814). This letter contains the celebrated '3 or 4 Families in a Country Village...' definitive of her own practice. She continues to remark on the talents of Scott, this time noticing his emergence as a novelist. Her humour is always present, and she observes that he has 'no business to write novels'; she certainly means to dislike Waverley, though she fears that she will succumb to its appeal (28 September 1814). However, she can wax satirical about lesser novelists and their romantic excesses, saying that she will write an imitation of a novel called 'Self-Control' in which her heroine will not merely go down an American river in a boat 'by herself, she shall cross the Atlantic in the same way' (November or December 1814). Then she has a natural pride in the interest of the Prince Regent in her writings and thus the resultant dedication of *Emma* to him.

There is also the wonderful disclaimer when his librarian asks her to write a novel about a clergyman. She considers that she is totally ill-fitted for the task, and her ironic tone shows how she puts herself down for her lack of a classical education, diminishes her own capacity and at the same time shows by the controlled, balanced, comic-spirited nature of her reply, that she is happily cognisant of her own limitations (11 December 1815). The words 'unlearned and uninformed' have provoked comment ever since they were published, but since we now know the range and the variety of Jane Austen's reading, this simulated modesty (or conditioned fun) shows the way she rejected anything which did not arise from her own wishes. Clarke continued his own unwelcome literary attentions, and she was forced to decline an opportunity to write a novel about the House of Saxe-Cobourg.

Her brother Edward was the recipient of her famous definition of her own method and range – 'the little bit (two Inches wide) of ivory' – on which she worked to so little effect in her own mind. But the letters begin to show the sadness of the illusion that she believes she is recovering her strength. They show too her delight in the letters she receives from Fanny Knight (20 February 1817); gradually one suspects she begins to be fully aware of the real state of her health. She feels that she will never be 'blooming' again, and wrily comments that illness 'is a dangerous Indulgence' at her age (23 March 1817). We recognize the nature of the smile here, and also the courage that informs it. Some of these later letters have a religious tone, as might be expected, and a warm recognition of those who have cared for her so tenderly. Even as late as March 1817, she records her pleasure at receiving £20 for the second edition of *Sense and Sensibility*.

Letters, even when there are gaps of long periods, as here, constitute the truest biography we can have. They reveal her close relationship with her family, especially Cassandra, and they reflect, as Chapman points out, the current epistolary practices and conventions. They show the liveliness of her mind and her down-to-earth acceptance of her own lot. Consider her definition of luxury – 'to sit in idleness over a good fire in a well-proportioned room' (8 November 1800), or this brilliant anticipation of Wilde – 'I have always maintained the importance of Aunts' (30 October 1815). They do much to fill in the outline: the wit, the asperity, the family love and concern, the moods which show generosity of spirit and those which are tetchy and occasionally ill-natured, all cohere to reveal the personality behind the writing.

6

Deepening Appraisals

Marvin Mudrick's *Jane Austen: Irony as Defense and Discovery* (1952; 1968 printing) has deservedly become a classic of Jane Austen criticism. He maintains that her characteristic defence throughout her work is irony, while she set out 'to sharpen and expose all the incongruities between form and fact, all the delusions intrinsic to conventional art and conventional society'. This statement sufficiently indicates the sophisticated nature of Mudrick's appraisal. He suggests that her personal irony, for instance, in her letters, is largely employed in the service of comedy, but that it 'had to overflow into some larger, formal medium', hence the novels. But it is early employed, through the mockery of 'the lachrymose novel in letters', in *Love and Freindship*. He adds that her 'having demolished the values of bad art, it ends as a criticism of life'. Mudrick's overview even includes the young Jane Austen's 'History of England', where he feels she disposes 'of history as of another unverifiable world'.

There is some superb examination in the chapter on *Northanger Abbey*; Mudrick holds that the ironic mode 'overtly juxtaposes the Gothic and the bourgeois worlds, and allows them to comment on each other'. This is extended definitively by 'The parody of a novel must itself be a novel: the novelist who shows what is artistically irrelevant and improbable must at the same time show what is relevant and probable'. The technical and functional emphasis is changed: Mudrick says that Henry Tilney, in fact, is given much of what had previously been the authorial function, that is, to employ the author's irony as criticism of society's conventions and, of course, the conventions of the kind of literature which are their equivalent. In his examination of the minor characters, Mudrick finds that John Thorpe has reversed or contrasted Gothic qualities; when he returns to Henry Tilney, he indicates that the latter's function is to 'unify the novel from within....'.

Mudrick develops his arguments consistently, believing that there is still an element of parody in *Sense and Sensibility* and elsewhere, which Jane Austen uses as 'the easiest irony'. He acknowledges that she moves towards a considered appraisal of the individual, and that in *Sense and Sensibility* personality is interpreted, so much so that in Elinor, who obviously has her author's approval, 'The views of author and reader begin to diverge'. One is inclined to credit this and to give it an ironic emphasis which goes beyond the author's intention. Mudrick rightly notes that 'Marianne's notion of sensibility remains; and we have yet learned nothing to make it appear trivial or invalid, or seriously inadequate as a criterion of human value'. There is irony in Elinor's misjudgement of Willoughby for she makes the mistake of considering him an eminently eligible bachelor (Mudrick believes that Marianne sees the 'potential Willoughby' clearly). Allied to his insight, Mudrick has the virtue of a refreshing directness on occasion, as when he says 'If Edward Ferrars is dull, Colonel Brandon is a vacuum'. Sometimes there is an irony beyond irony in Jane Austen: 'Against her own moral will and conscious artistic purpose, the creator makes her creature wholly sympathetic – because, one must conclude, Marianne represents an unacknowledged depth of her author's spirit'. We may recognize the sympathy, but reject the subjectivity. Marianne's sensibility, like Elinor's sense, is searchingly probed: the author's spirit is present in both, though covert in one and open in the other, yet both are evidence of a wide tolerance.

Identifications between Elizabeth Bennet and her author are relatively obvious, but I don't think that we have to accept that her judgement is as sharply ironic as her creator's. It is true to say that Elizabeth misjudges, and that in doing so she underpins the title, the morality, and of course, the major part of the plot. Mudrick allows that Elizabeth underestimates the pressures on Charlotte Lucas, for he believes (as does the reader, I suggest), that Charlotte has steeled herself to ignore the insensitivities of her husband. He underlines Elizabeth's recognition of her father (this constitutes 'discovery'), allowing for the fact that marriages are based on sexual attraction as well as on economics. They represent, finally, the yielding up of choice, 'an irremediable self-degradation and defeat'. Again, one is aware of the overstatement. In *Pride and Prejudice*, irony is used to discriminate between social stereotypes and individuals possessed of self-will.

Lady Susan and *The Watsons* are combed for irony, but it is on *Mansfield Park* that Mudrick's investigation sheds its most searching and uncompromising light. His chapter 'The Triumph of Gentility' stresses personal 'choice of allegiance; and the action of the novel is a collision of worlds'. In essence, Mudrick is appraising the author's acceptance of the Mansfield standards, and this of course involves Fanny's acceptance of them too: 'It is always clear to her that Sir Thomas and Edmund – the guardian spirits of Mansfield Park – are good and just'. Once again one feels that another layer of irony is present somewhere in the author's unconscious (or conscious) conception, for it may be argued that Sir Thomas is a failed parent (and perhaps husband), that Edmund is largely blind (witness his feelings for Mary Crawford), and that Fanny is blind to these faults because of her acquired status. Mudrick says that '*Mansfield Park* was to be a novel vindicating the ethical foundation of Jane Austen's world', but if this is so, one can only suggest that she was unaware of the double-edged sword she was wielding, and I find this hard to accept. Nonetheless, there are still some considered statements in this section which compel our attention and respect, such as, 'The Crawfords are the only characters in the novel whose source and mode of expression is irony'.

In his chapter on *Emma*, Mudrick refers back to 'the uneasy stiffness of *Mansfield Park*', which is a comment on his own narrow-beamed consideration of it. Jane Austen is in a relaxed frame throughout *Emma*, where she is deft and distinct in all she does. Mudrick's character-appraisal of Emma emphasizes that she is always appealing even when she is capricious in behaviour and attitude (I do not believe this is the case early in the novel). Here though, Mudrick's perceptions are enlightened, as when he observes that she is moved to change the lives of other people but not the lives of her father and herself, for her life only mirrors her father's, which is an insubstantial equivalent of her own. It certainly seems to be and explains so much of Emma's motivation and practice. Mudrick feels that Frank Churchill is cautious, covering his essential egocentricity by the casual charm he exudes, and there is some truth in the assertion that Emma 'plays God' because of her inability 'to commit herself humanly'. There is a fine examination of the ironies of plot and structure and the 'deceptiveness of surface' with 'Charm' as 'most often the signal of wit adrift from feeling'. Mudrick's style is rarely consonant with that of his author. The book is uneven but memorable both for its bias and its insights. For example, he says that 'The new element in *Persuasion* is personal feeling'. In relation to Anne Elliot, we know what he means, but the statement seems to refute earlier evidences of identification and sympathetic affinity. He also says that the conflict in this novel is not given ironically, and that it is between 'the feudal remnant, conscious of its tradition, and the rising middle class, conscious of its vitality, at the turn of the nineteenth century'. It is as if he feels the need to depart from his self-imposed prescription, though in the sequence of his own study it is a little late to do so. Moreover, I don't think that we can admit that *Persuasion* 'shows the author closely attentive to personal feeling and to economic tensions for the first time'. Mudrick is stimulating because he paved the way for more extensive investigations and also because he writes with his eye on the novels. He makes us blink, in sudden fellow-feeling or disagreement, by his definitions of irony in its various forms and variant usages through Jane Austen's work.

The sub-title of Andrew Wright's *Jane Austen's Novels*

(1957) is *A Study in Structure*, and the chapter headings make it clear that he is concerned primarily with what he calls 'Materials and Themes', the 'Points of View' which constitute 'Narrative Management', the structures of the characterization and Jane Austen's 'Styles'. He establishes that she has a firm sense of her own boundaries, something rare in novel practice in her own time. There follows a survey of opinions from Scott onwards. Wright is concerned to demonstrate her themes and is dismissive of the 'money' theory, and also of Daiches' idea – that she was 'in a sense a Marxist before Marx'. Wright finds three levels of meaning in the novels – the local, the broadly allegorical, and the ironic. She omits the lower classes, and hardly considers the aristocracy, except by way of satire, for she is concerned with the country gentry, and men only appear in the company of women.

Mansfield Park is seen as didactic: 'it is a treatise on education'. *Emma* is seen as a novel of instruction, while the 'theme of *Persuasion* is Overpersuasion'. All her work is ironic within his definition of the term, 'the juxtaposition, in fact, of two mutually incompatible views of life'.

She 'omnisciently presents insights into her characters', moving, as with Fanny Price, from intelligent neutral observer to intimate identification in her heroine's consciousness. Sometimes she comments indirectly, putting forward 'a view which cannot represent that of any of her characters, and which may not be her own'. This, of course, is one of her ironic modes. Even when she uses direct comment the reader has to gauge whether the views of the author are being given or whether this is a deliberate pose. The celebrated 'guilt and misery' reference in *Mansfield Park* is re-examined in the light of this.

Commonsense in her works is set beside the maxims she so often uses, but 'hovering about every single piece of homely wisdom is the ironic qualification'. Sometimes there is a wryness about the generalizations. Wright comments on her dramatic instincts, citing the confrontation between Elizabeth and Lady Catherine in the shrubbery, and her brilliant capacity here in the foreshortening of conversations. He links the dramatic mode to the third person reportage which complements it. He pinpoints what is now the obvious, the fact that marriage proposals are recorded and not dramatized. His best work in this section, however, is on 'interior disclosures', for example, in Elizabeth's reactions to Darcy's letter, which contains 'artistic objectivity', to the ability to get inside the minds of unsympathetic characters, a further extension of her structural grasp.

In dealing with character, she concentrates essentially on interrelationships. In her individuals, however, Jane Austen ensures that each 'person has a function, yet every one comes alive'. For Wright, dramatic irony plays the central part in her presentation of character. In *Sense and Sensibility*, for example, 'both girls have dimensions beyond the terms of the title'. Edward and Willoughby are of little interest but are functionally important to the appraisal of Elinor and Marianne. Willoughby's arrival at Cleveland Wright finds unforgiveable. The important thing in *Northanger Abbey* is Catherine's 'emergence as a human being', and then 'a human being of good sense'. Henry Tilney is the 'only one of Jane Austen's heroes who shares her ironic viewpoint, the only one who ever threatens the primacy of a heroine'. Darcy and Wickham subserve the ironic theme of *Pride and Prejudice*, and irony is absent from *Mansfield Park* in the presentation of Fanny and Edmund; the novel itself is 'uncomplicatedly didactic'. Emma, on the other hand, is 'the victim of her own illusions: she creates a world, but it is not the real world'. Wright includes much summary, in between quotations and commentary, emphasizing his points. It means that the arguments, most of which seem self-evident, are simply followed through.

The section on 'Styles' has some refreshing subtlety, with a close look at language which, like Fielding's, Wright believes, is 'too heavy for the structure it must support – and so the diction casts the shadow of suspicion on the validity of the thought'. In the same way, she shows her 'sharply critical attitude towards the Bingley sisters'. Sometimes single words tincture a paragraph with irony: in the later works she produces over-elaborate sentences for her 'tiresome talkers'. She uses understatement in addition, and multiple negatives

are employed by characters whom she dislikes, also, ironically, by favoured characters like Catherine Morland. Burlesque (as in *Northanger Abbey*) is reflected in misusages,
while words, such as, 'remarkable' are used to convey the
opposite; she is the mistress of the anti-climactic phrase and
her styles underpin her irony. Wright's sensible and modest
criticism is a handbook introduction to the main Austen
modes.

Brian Southam's name occurs regularly throughout this
summary of scholarship and criticism, and here we are
concerned with the pioneering investigation of his *Jane
Austen's Literary Manuscripts: A Study of the novelist's development through the surviving papers* (1964). It is about
her writing 'outside the major works', and is 'in part' a
supplement to biography, recording the influence of her family on her, but also indicating her reading, some important
chronology, corrections and revisions. Southam feels that her
achievement as a novelist, her dedication to her art, was 'won
through many years of highly conscious experiment'. Like
Tanner (see pp. 113-18), he sees *Sanditon* as complex and
refined, indicating its 'figurative and symbolic devices' which
makes Jane Austen indeed 'a writer of the nineteenth century'. It is with generous spirit that he pays tribute to the
critical work of Mary Lascelles and Marvin Mudrick.

First of all he deals with 'the Writing of the Juvenilia',
noting incidentally the family opposition to the printing of
these works, perhaps because they 'contain a lively strain of
humour offensive to Victorian taste'. He further notes 'the
gradual change as the young writer began to turn from
burlesque entertainment to experiment in the techniques of
fiction'. He then records – it is his main thesis – the consistency and continuity of her work, right through to *Sanditon*,
which he finds 'deeply grounded in literary satire'.

He asserts from his evidence that both family environment
and her reading fed into burlesque, her earliest form of
writing, and a precocious one. He refers to the influence of
Cassandra, whose 'sharp, satirical miniature to "The History
of England" survives to show us that the sisters were well
matched'. After the arrival of Eliza Feuillide, 'a little

dramatic company' came into being again. Southam says that we need to be aware of the 'stratum of lost or hidden meaning' which is there despite the fact that those that gave rise to it – the family and the parish, for example – have passed away.

The other usual influences – Dr Johnson, Richardson and Cowper – are noted, and he asserts that Jane Austen believed that 'literature is properly a means to truth, and that truth is to be found in the realms of common sense and real life, not in the romantic delusions of sentimentalism'. He carefully examines the dating of the transcripts, and feels that Jane Austen's continued interest in what she wrote 'is to be explained by its importance as a kind of traditional family literature'. He then undertakes an invaluable critical study of the *Juvenilia*, saying that Jane Austen's theme throughout is 'the need to distinguish between reality and illusion', and he believes that among the last of the *Juvenilia* the most important works are those in which 'the burlesque element is subordinated to realistic social comedy'. The early material embraces 'broad farcical comedy' and 'the studied formality of the sentimental language and behaviour of the characters'. There are certainly glimpses of her later manner and assurance in the 'occasional succinct aphorism or finely-turned comment'.

The examination of what he calls 'The Middle Work' (1790-1), traces this development, *Love and Freindship* demonstrating that her 'burlesque becomes a satire on affectation'. In addition she illustrates 'the mishandling of the letter as a narrative form'. In her 'History of England' Jane Austen is set on proving that 'popularised history is as false to the nature of reality as the pictures of life given in the sentimental novel'. I said 'invaluable' as an estimate of Southam's work here (and elsewhere): he is, I believe, always alert to the connections, without straining. His own saturation in Jane Austen's novels and life is evident, so that his deductions carry a weight of sympathetic authority. His third section is on 'The Last of the Juvenilia' (1892-3), which he finds generally disappointing. He makes an exception for the fragment of 'Catherine', feeling that it 'is suited to the opening of a full-scale work'. He further believes that it is the first statement of her artistic principles, which are: to keep within the 'bounds of her experience' and to insist on 'truth of representation'. Presumably she did not complete it because she realized that she was not being successful with her heroine. He next considers *Lady Susan* and 'The Lost Originals', feeling that *Lady Susan* is a return 'to the less demanding form of the correspondence novel'. Indeed it is, but with what compensations, as Southam is quick to demonstrate: 'As an individual character-study Lady Susan is remarkable and fascinating, a figure who would not be out of place in the pages of Wycherley or Congreve'. It is overstatement but perhaps only marginally so, for it is certainly true that she has 'the commanding personality of a brilliant hypocrite', and that the work 'reads as an autonomous and complete creation'. He reprints here in full Cassandra's note and the dates of composition, pointing out that Chapman's chronologies 'remain uncorrected'. Southam goes on to suggest that 'the extant version of *Northanger Abbey* is close to its original form'.

With *The Watsons* Southam strikes a bold and independent note: 'The account of the Watson family and their neighbours is the most severe and pessimistic view of society to be found in all Jane Austen's work'. He also looks at 'The Plan of a Novel', which hits out at distortion, melodrama and lack of realism in contemporary stories. He feels that this should be read in conjunction with the letters of advice to Anna, maintaining that once again here is evidence of the consistency of Jane Austen's critical attitude and her own practice (concerned with offering her readers a relaxed and natural observation of life, derived from everyday experience). He stresses her artistic integrity, considering critically the two chapters of *Persuasion*, the revision and the original, seeing the former as evidence of her ability to re-work material both with care and inspiration. His praise for *Sanditon* is in some ways close to the conclusions of Tony Tanner, which it precedes. He feels the vigour and power of the writing, with the group which is under closest scrutiny marked by febrile energy. He develops the idea that it is in *Sanditon* that Jane Austen uses potent imagery, although her range is limited. He goes further, finding a possible biographical reason for the nature of the book, which he sees as a revolt against her own sickness, 'the artist's lively and energetic compensation for the state of her body' (it is typical of Southam to state what is so likely with an appropriate modesty).

In an Appendix, he denigrates Q.D. Leavis' 'A Critical Theory of Jane Austen's Writings' (from *Scrutiny* 1941, 1942, 1944) which is really an attempt to establish the originals in Jane Austen's fiction. Southam refers to the *Memoir* where Jane Austen stated that 'it was her desire to create, not to reproduce'. The arguments he uses in support of this are conclusive. Inevitably she drew from life, as great artists do, but any original is submerged in the intellectual and imaginative creativity which encompasses the character. Southam's study tells us much more about Jane Austen both as a person and as an artist than any popular biography could do, since it draws on what she wrote and how she was at the critical and particularly formative periods of her life.

W.A. Craik's *Jane Austen: The Six Novels* (1965; reprinted 1968) is an unpretentious study. In her Introduction she says 'Her greatness lies in the way in which she combines the artist and the moralist; hers is a perfect, because a natural, reconciliation of the two'. This reasonable statement indicates the low-key nature of the book, which initially stresses Jane Austen's simplicity, something which succeeding criticism has turned into subtlety. She finds a limitation in *Northanger Abbey*, where Jane Austen appears to be split by the pull of two intentions – 'of literary burlesque and of social and moral comment', which 'come eventually into opposition during the events at Northanger'. We might consider that these co-exist in harmony, given the structure of the novel and the nature of its action. Catherine is carefully analysed, but again Miss Craik feels that 'A fault of the plot is that as Catherine's character becomes more psychologically interesting it bcomes less so as a literary force'. This is muddled, to say the least, particularly when she goes on to say 'the action always appears to rise out of character'. She categorizes Jane Austen's style as 'easy, unaffected and professional', and rightly believes 'One of the greatest pleasures in her novels is conversation'. The discussion of *Sense and Sensibility* includes the now accepted view that Marianne has been found more attractive than Elinor by most readers, 'which Jane Austen clearly did not intend', and she follows this by asserting that 'Elinor is an isolated heroine' whose 'opinions discipline the events: she gives the rational view of them which the reader should share'. This emphasis perhaps indicates how dated the comment is. Here, when subtlety and its acceptance replace simplicity, one sees Jane Austen providing the balanced appraisal of her heroines, which the title of the novel suggests. Miss Craik feels that character and plot are equally important in a Jane Austen novel, and says that 'Irony is beginning to take its place as one of her finest skills, as a most economical means of delineating character, and as an accurate means of revealing states of mind'. This is, I feel, sufficiently obvious, but it does need reiterating.

Elizabeth Bennet 'is perceptive even when she misinterprets what she hears', and the genuine advance in *Pride and Prejudice* is seen in the fact that 'Character, narrative and conversation are virtually inseparable'. One is inclined to feel that 'narrative' is not complete enough, and that either 'omniscience' or 'commentary' should be added to show the density of the texture. Another comment here hints at what Barbara Hardy was to examine so well in her study of Jane Austen (see pp. 89-91): 'The action is organized not only by what happens, but by where it happens; the place itself is relevant to what occurs'. Of *Mansfield Park* she observes 'While her novels are essentially serious in intention, this comes closest of them all to being sober in treatment'. Again, I feel, we are aware that limited language cannot convey the *essential* texture of Jane Austen's writing and achievement. It is true to say that 'Fanny is the pivot of the action rather than an active heroine' (and neatly put), but it seems quirky to suggest that *Mansfield Park* 'is yet not so completely satisfying even as *Sense and Sensibility* though its parts are so much superior'. She demonstrates the quality of those parts so well, stressing the effect of environment on character, noting that Mary Crawford makes 'an agreeable change

from the restraint of Fanny and the hypocrisy of Mansfield
as a whole'. *Emma* calls forth an independent judgement,
since it is Jane Austen's 'best and most misunderstood work'.
Here 'hints at links between characters seem as inex-
haustible as they are in life'. Character presentation is fuller
than in any of the other novels, and Miss Bates' irrelevances
are, in fact, often 'relevant to some later matter'. *Persuasion*
shows Jane Austen 'moving towards a more introspective
kind of writing'. Throughout Miss Craik's discussion there
are sober and rational emphases, but the criticism never
takes fire from its subject.

Howard Babb examined stylistic aspects of her work in
Jane Austen's Novels: The Fabric of Dialogue (1967). The
approach is chronological, but the initial investigation of
style (for example, 'how typically Jane Austen accumulates
nouns referring to concepts'), shows that they are there at
the introduction of each character and also in the emotional
exchanges. Related to these are her general statements,
which often suggest 'a firm conviction that society's judgements, the substance of the generalisations, are reliable'; she
also 'generalises in the interests of propriety'. Her use of
metaphors is sparing, and these tend to be 'figures so familiar
that their meanings have been circumscribed and their emotions carefully subdued'. Of course, some metaphors are
employed with ironic and parodic weight. Finally, there is the
rhetorical aspect of her work, where she 'recreates a flow of
fact and sensation'. Babb cites as example an early description of the Middletons, where the 'rhetoric both organises and
energises an adverse judgement' of them; her style 'con-
structs a version of reality'.

The section on *Sense and Sensibility* ('Symmetrical De-
signs') is evident for the most part, though there is some
astute evaluation of Willoughby's language ('For him emotion is something to be professed by means of rhetoric, irony,
and diction – they are tools to indulge it – but not to be
thoroughly acted upon'). *Northanger Abbey* has the Babb
word-awareness in the sub-title of the chapter ('Parody, Ped-
agogy, and the Play of Feeling)', which defines accurately the
overall concerns of the novel. He stresses in particular, 'the

dialogues between Catherine and Henry' as dramatizing Jane Austen's theme. The emphasis in the discussion of *Pride and Prejudice* is on its vitality, for it has a 'vibrancy and a rich dramatic texture'. There is particular praise for the successful portrayal of Darcy, and in this novel 'our point of view is much more subtly managed' than in the earlier novels. For example, she hides Darcy's real character from us for much of the novel, as it is in the latter part of the novel that her characters develop. Consider Elizabeth's putting down of Lady Catherine 'by discriminating between wishes, facts, and moral obligations'. Babb defines the theme of *Pride and Prejudice* as 'judging from behaviour and behaving with judgement', (meaning an ability to distinguish what is real from what is professed). He looks closely at an exchange between Elizabeth and Darcy near the end of the novel to show how far they have developed over its course: Darcy discovers the need to employ 'gracious display', while Elizabeth discovers that her judgement of Darcy was derived from false reasoning. Babb finds *Mansfield Park* of a piece with the rest of Jane Austen's work, though he feels that it is noticeably colder in tone; at the same time, he recognizes the skill with which Fanny's consciousness is revealed to us. The conversations, as always, spell out the nature of the characters, and the author's moral judgement is brought to bear on the misjudgements of her creatures. Mrs Norris is obtuse, while Sir Thomas stands corrected, particularly in his support of Maria's decision to marry Rushworth, despite the fact that he – Sir Thomas – knows that she is indifferent to him. The minor figures, such as Fanny's parents, for example, are flawed by their self-interest. Edmund's moral descent with regard to Mary Crawford is reflected in his behaviour and his rhetoric, and he is also blind with regard to Fanny.

Emma shows Jane Austen's sophisticated use of irony which is developed through a sequence of misjudgements, right through to Emma's realization of what she most wants. Though the novel is based on Emma's perspective, there is one significant shift to Knightley's perspective in order to 'place' Jane Fairfax and Frank Churchill more accurately.

Babb feels that Emma is a snob, condescending and self-elev-
ating, and here is the major irony of the novel – the fact that
Emma herself is guilty of radical misjudgement with regard
to her own feelings. Through the particularities of the Box
Hill incident she is forced to see her real self, and the dialogue
records her changes in behaviour. There is also much praise
for the climactic scene between Emma and Knightley.

Babb gives a fine analysis of feeling in *Persuasion*, a
defence of the assimilation of William Elliot into the plot, and
has special glances at manipulation. Anne is able to absorb
the different experiences with patience, tolerance and endurance. Babb's work is sensitive and direct; one of his conclusions seems to me to be incontrovertible: it is, that the main
motif of Jane Austen's work is to demonstrate the 'disparity
between appearance and reality'. This I believe to be true,
and her scenes and dialogues both dramatize the disparity
and emphasize the movements of reality.

Marghanita Laski's *Jane Austen and Her World* (1969) is
a useful volume to set beside Lord David Cecil's *Portrait*.
Superbly illustrated, it does what its title suggests – places
Jane Austen locally and more widely in the period context.
There is a competent summary of her reading and of her
cousin 'Eliza's contributions to their private theatricals'. Her
first writings are seen in relation to the social life of the
family in the neighbourhood. The nature of the Austen family
is shown, and there are a number of shrewd comments, for
instance, our lack of knowledge of Jane's comments on important events when she and Cassandra were together.
Indeed, she feels that Jane Austen's 'girlish love' for Tom
Lefroy should be defined in just that way.

There are neat links made between the letters and the
early writings, and Miss Laski opts for an early date for *Lady
Susan* (the watermarked paper 1805 does not impress her,
and she suggests that this is a fair copy). She describes the
years at Bath as 'unhappy and dull', but records the happy
and joking way in which Jane Austen approached the decision to settle in Chawton, even flirting with the idea (for Mrs
Knight's benefit) of marrying the bachelor Rector.

Miss Laski feels that the gap in letter-writing between

1809 and 1811 'is due rather to pleasure than to disaster'. The inspirational effect of Chawton on her writing, despite her many domestic duties, is given a considered stress, as is her visit to London in the early months of 1811.

The secret that Jane Austen was the author of *Pride and Prejudice* was given away by her brother Henry, and Miss Laski obviously enjoys telling us that Jane Austen's own delight in her characters 'continued far beyond the limits of the novels in which she confined them'. Miss Laski finds little difficulty in accepting that *Mansfield Park* is about 'ordination', and she embraces the question of originals in *Persuasion*, neatly recording Jane Austen's own remark about Anne Elliot to Fanny Knight – 'You *may* perhaps like the Heroine, as she is almost too good for me'. Miss Laski closes this fluent introduction to Jane Austen by printing a letter from Fanny Knight ('the delight of her aunt's life') written much later, saying 'it is very true that Aunt Jane for various circumstances was not so *refined* as she ought to have been for her *talent*' and 'Aunt Jane was too clever to put aside all possible signs of "common-ness" (if such an expression is allowable) and teach herself to be more refined, at least in intercourse with people in general'. The vulgar snobbery – and the human envy – are tantalizing but inconclusive.

K.C. Phillipps' *Jane Austen's English* (1970) is an intriguing investigation of particularities of her language usage and style, with some incidental critical evaluation which enhances his own presentation. For example, he registers her differentiation of character through dialogue, citing the 'amorphous syntax' of Miss Bates; Lucy Steele is socially categorized through her language, written or spoken, since good grammar and good breeding are equated in Jane Austen. There is a deft weighing of her use of abstract nouns, her reliance on 18th-century 'terms like *liberality, propriety, delicacy* on the one hand' and 'the distillation of a more dramatic and realistic language from the best spoken English she heard about her' on the other.

In evaluating her vocabulary, Phillipps says that she 'had a keen eye for the illogical expression' and was particularly severe on vague or slang terms. 'Nice' and 'horrid' get the benefit of her undercutting irony in *Northanger Abbey*, for she found 'novel-slang' abhorrent, ridiculed loose syntax, vulgar turns of phrase, over-technical vocabulary and the affectation of foreign phrases (witness Mrs Elton's *caro sposo*). Changes in the weight of words are recorded: for example, 'genius' has a 'milder quality' than that expressed today, whereas 'tease' was stronger. Another difference is seen in 'indulge' and 'indulgence', which have 'disparaging overtones' today, but were used by Jane Austen to convey enjoyment; similarly 'peculiar' was used as we now use 'particular'. Phillipps asserts that 'Jane Austen's use of a word is nearer to the etymological sense than our own', giving as examples, 'secure', 'free from care, untroubled'.

She uses a number of key words, such as 'elegance', with its various shades of differentiation. David Lodge (in *The Language of Fiction*), had already recorded that 'principle' is a key word in *Mansfield Park*, while Phillipps himself says that in *Emma* 'superior' is found 'at least thirty times'. When Jane Austen uses the word 'mind' she is defining 'the basic and essential foundation of the whole personality'. Interestingly, he records the incidence of financial and taxation metaphors, though he acknowledges that 'In general, she preferred her metaphors dead'. Jane Austen balances abstract and concrete language, and she is 'a mistress of the *double-entendre*'. There are some words, such as 'engage', which are 'more elastic in meaning, and more versatile in construction, than they are today'. The language of social intercourse figures largely, with derogatory epithets such as 'rattle', 'quiz', and 'puppy' stigmatizing character. They have passed out of usage, while Jane Austen's 'sensations' is now equivalent to our 'feelings'. Other specialized vocabulary has now dated or disappeared, such as 'fish' from the French *fiche*, a small piece of ivory or bone in her time, used instead of money for keeping account in games of chance. There is too vocabulary used of the weather, for example, 'open', which means free from frost. Jane Austen's innovations include 'coze' (a pleasant chat), used in *Mansfield Park* and in her letters, and 'sweep', which is a curved carriage drive. Her sentence structure involves the use of expanded tenses, and

Phillipps refers particularly to her 'curious and rather frequent use of the expanded present participle', as in 'being going on so well', 'being dancing with him', and 'being acting a part'. The infinitive is sometimes 'used absolutely with exclamatory force', for instance, in *Persuasion* where we find 'An ancient family to be so driven away!' All great writers are guilty of grammatical errors but Jane Austen uses mistakes as character comments. This frequently takes the form of a deliberate disregard of concord, as in the vulgar 'how *was* they to live upon that' (*Sense and Sensibility*) and 'Here *is* Morland and I come to stay' (*Northanger Abbey*). The superlative degree regularly occurs when only two things are compared, as in 'Mr Martin may be the *richest* of the two' (*Emma*). Another idiosyncrasy is the omitted preposition, and Phillipps also includes formal modes of address which are characteristic of the novels, underlining the solecisms or omissions which are again critical of character, as in Mrs Elton's familiar use of 'Knightley' in *Emma*. Phillipps' analysis sits lightly and attractively: we feel its depth, but there are no pedantic overtones. Like Jane Austen's writing, it is at once charming, accurate and incisive.

7

Centenary Elevations

Some words of Jane Austen (1973) by Stuart Tave is a modest but important book. It is subtle, close and limpidly clear. In his first section he notes that both foolish and intelligent characters 'reshape the space and time they inhabit to make it a creation of their own wishes'. He notes the chronology of the novels, which 'is usually worked out with a quiet but unfailing care', and exactitude is of the essence: 'time moves softly but certainly, as a natural and inevitable line of life'.

For Jane Austen, and for her characters, words are 'life's necessary fulfilling form', of course, open to abuse by someone like Mr Collins, 'an absolute master at separating words from their meanings'. Some language is inadequate 'because reality itself becomes indefinable', as with Sir Edward Denham in *Sanditon*. The relation of language to character is brilliantly put at the end of the first section ('Limitations and Definitions'):

> Strong feelings rise in her characters, rightly and necessarily at moments of crisis, with pleasures and pains beyond what they have ever felt: the characteristic accompaniment of this increase of feeling is an increase in articulateness; they must often struggle for it but their stature is in proportion to their willingness to try for it and their eventual success in achieving the brightness of command.

From Catherine Morland to Anne Elliot we register the truth

of the above statement. And there is some shrewd analysis – expansive and stimulating – on the heroines. *Northanger Abbey* effectively destroys romance since Catherine's hopes are rarely realized, but what is important is her capacity to learn. Moreover, there is a development from artlessness to artfulness following her experiences at Northanger. She affects to be surprised when in fact what happens is what she secretly expected. She begins to make observations, becomes more fully aware, draws inferences and even comes to conclusions, such as the knowledge that 'To live well in common life is uncommon'. Tave suggests that she acquires a greater dignity, a measure of her creator's achievement in her presentation.

Turning to Marianne, we sometimes find 'amusement', since what she thinks of as her power – her sensibility – is really weakness. She creates a sensibility which is not there in Willoughby. Tave feels that our interest in her derives from the fact that she *is* superior, but that she abuses rather than uses her quality of superiority because she is not rational or truthful with herself. She is also lacking in tolerance, and she simply does not understand the nature of what is occurring. Tave stresses that *Sense and Sensibility* is the story of Elinor, and that it comes to us through her. His analysis turns the readily common denigrations of Elinor on their heads, for he feels that her feelings are much greater than those of Marianne's, and that her efforts – in every direction – are greater too. He feels that 'exertion' is the key-word here and the mainspring of her morality: it is the public sign of her private searchings and decisions. The key-words in the consideration of *Pride and Prejudice* are 'amiable' and 'agreeable': Elizabeth's happiness is built on her capacity to recognize an amiable man when she sees him; when she finally comes to an appreciation of Darcy's worth she says 'He is perfectly amiable'. Tave feels that this is 'astonishing' and 'daring' given the context (and I believe it is indeed). Tave's demonstration of its truthfulness is exact and reflects the quality of his close appraisal. He points out another related word, 'affection', and again we are shown its variant usages. Tave cites a letter to Fanny Knight in which Jane Austen observes 'Anything is to be preferred or endured rather than marrying without Affection'. There is a growing affection between Elizabeth and Darcy over a period of time. 'Mortification' is given a detailed commentary; 'liveliness', at least in the case of Elizabeth, represents the superiority of her spirit and awareness, placing her in control of 'the possibilities of life'. There is a revealing section on the 'ironic reversals' of Henry Crawford's career, while Tave suggests that Fanny herself is the recipient of Jane Austen's irony in revealing particular weaknesses. There is some detail on Emma conceiving a world in her own imagination. Thus 'fancy' is one of the words most employed here (Emma is an 'imaginist'), and a lively imagination makes for power, not always well-directed, as Emma demonstrates in her own misjudgements and interferings. The word 'elegance' carries true and false associations, aptly contrasted in the people and personalities of Emma and Mrs Elton, though Jane Fairfax appears to possess the outward and inward variety. However, she lacks – for obvious reasons of plot necessity – 'ease', something also lacking in a character like Darcy. Frank Churchill possesses it deceptively, while Emma is not really as much at ease as she thinks she is. There is a penetrating commentary on the most important episode in *Emma*, the Box Hill party: here Tave shrewdly notes that Emma seems to have all the important words at her command as definitions of her selfhood – for example, 'liveliness', 'ease', 'wit', 'judgement' – but in truth 'she is never further from all she imagines'.

In *Persuasion* Anne is at the centre of everything, although Jane Austen has told us significantly 'her word had no weight'. She listens and looks, she hears but is not heard by others, and the important element in the revised chapter of *Persuasion* is the new ability of Captain Wentworth to hear her. She faces 'opposed forces' but never loses her capacity to judge rightly; her integrity remains inviolable. With Captain Wentworth knowledge begins when he is overpowered by the effects of Louisa's accident. He has to learn about himself before he can learn to understand Anne and begin to rid himself of the feelings about the past which have conditioned his responses to her. Tave's analysis of Anne is characteristic of his own subtlety of response and of Jane Austen's subtlety of presentation. Anne 'has what seem to be specifically feminine virtues of submission and patience, of feeling, and yet she has what may seem to be the masculine virtues of activity and usefulness, of exertion', but 'she makes these distinctions irrelevant to her comprehensive greatness'.

This study, which has its own qualities of greatness, is referred to respectfully by modern scholars in passing, but seems largely unrecorded in their own commentaries. It is direct, finely and succinctly written, almost in the Austen image, not through imitation or parody but through sympathetic association and intellectual identification. If Mary Lascelles makes so much modern Jane Austen criticism possible, then Stuart Tave implements her principles with discipline and imagination. For him, familiarity is knowledge, and that knowledge is shared with us.

D.D. Devlin's *Jane Austen and Education* (1975) is one of a number of books undertaking a detailed study of an aspect of her work. The breadth of the conception here is at once apparent: 'Education, for the heroines, is a process through which they come to see clearly themselves and their conduct, and by this new vision or insight become better people'. In other words they acquire 'true knowledge'. *Mansfield Park* contains 'Jane Austen's most profound discussion of education; it is not the heroine who has to see clearly, but Edmund and his father. Fanny alone is truly aware...'. For Anne Elliot, on the other hand, there is the 'bitter process of education' which has occurred before the novel proper begins.

Devlin maintains that Jane Austen had certainly read Locke, and that he is a great influence on her: 'Locke insists that education must begin in infancy' and that 'virtue will be more easily acquired by private teaching'. His four great aims for education were 'virtue, wisdom, breeding and learning'. By contrast, non-education would be found in the delivery and content of almost everything uttered by Mr Collins, together with his idea of what constitutes forgiveness, plus 'the vapid truisms of Mary Bennet'. Locke's emphasis is on the moral development of the child, while 'To be virtuous is to see clearly'. There is an interesting emphasis on the fact that 'the Sage or Tutor appears in many eighteenth-century novels as a mentor-character'. Jane Austen herself is very aware of the 'nature—nurture problem' and, looking to the conclusions of the novels, it can be safely asserted that 'A happy marriage...guarantees the continuing education of both partners'.

It is Devlin's contention that Mary Crawford, for example, has been 'injured' by faulty education, while a telling quotation from *Mansfield Park* (ch. 48) shows Sir Thomas Bertram's sense of acknowledged failure: 'He feared that principle, active principle, had been wanting, that they had never been properly taught to govern their inclinations and tempers, by that sense of duty which alone can suffice'. Locke emphasized the importance of good habits of conduct, and Jane Austen also agrees with him 'that freedom is control of our passions and selfish impulses', but she finds 'that it is also clarification of vision'.

Devlin now proceeds to examine some of the fiction. He is directly relevant on *Lady Susan*, where the heroine 'does not understand the language of true feeling, and mistakes love for impudence'. Catherine (in *Northanger Abbey*), he says, has the 'moral toughness which is characteristic of all Jane Austen's heroines', while 'Darcy is, indirectly, Elizabeth's tutor; through his letter, in which he tells the truth, he comments by implication on Elizabeth's faults of prejudice and pride'. It is an interesting assertion, but maybe one should add that Elizabeth also educates Darcy into a greater social awareness, and that she mitigates his pride and prejudice (in that order) by the qualitative influence of her independence and vivacity. Devlin's sequence is somewhat curious. He now returns to the background again, discounting the idea that the third Earl of Shaftesbury is 'the chief philosophical presence in her work'. He sees Willoughby and Henry Crawford as 'Shaftesburian men of taste; they share his attitudes and catch his tone', and this obviously leads to the deduction that Jane Austen dislikes their attitudes. One of the most perceptive pieces of analysis arises from the fact that 'Shaftesbury does not find natural benevolence only in man, but in the natural world as well'. In the light of this,

Devlin examines Fanny's apostrophe to the world of nature in *Mansfield Park*, pointing out that she is not preaching adoration of the natural world but is looking at specifics – 'particular stars and particular consellations'. At the end of this section he measures the influence of Dr Johnson and Joseph Butler on Jane Austen, asserting that the theme of freedom for the individual and how it can be achieved is central in Jane Austen's fiction.

These remarks precede a full evaluation of the moral issues in *Mansfield Park*, with marriage always presented as the moral measure of the education of the individual, an index to 'disposition and character'. Thus, Mary Crawford's cynicism and snobbery are obvious moral faults, as well as self-ignorance: one might extend this to Edmund, but for Devlin he exemplifies the fact that manners rest on good principles. Fanny's freedom is shown at Sotherton and in the *Lovers' Vows* episode, and he notes that she is that rarity among the heroines, one whose gifts do not lie in talking so well as to be 'the best talker in the novel'. He goes further, rejecting Mudrick's idea that Jane Austen 'has conditioned the entire course of the narrative upon our acceptance of Sir Thomas's code', when in practice, she has undermined it. There is positive independence in Devlin's approach and, if the study is deliberately limited in range, it is nonetheless sharply revealing in its chosen areas.

Douglas Bush's *Jane Austen* (1975), in the centenary year, registers the benefits she has gained 'from the general advance of modern criticism from loose impressionism to precise analysis'. This emphasized 'the larger and deeper significance of her small themes' and established her as having 'a sane imagination at once realistic and detached'. He says she is 'an instinctive realist', describes her world as it is, and 'distinguishes between true and spurious gentility'. Moreover, although she avoids the overt immorality of 'guilt and misery', her novels are replete with what 'may be more corrosive and injurious, the common human faults of selfishness, insensitivity, insincerity, and the like'.

The competent summary of her life is followed by an equally precise evaluation of her early writings, among which he places *Lady Susan*, remarking on its 'relentless hardness which makes it unique in the Austen canon'. He then deals firstly with *Northanger Abbey* (it was the earliest completed of the novels) and praises its 'linear simplicity of design'. He adds that Gothic romance, however, 'threatens to warp moral judgement'. Bush feels, though, that the early parts of the novel are easily the best, with their 'dominant tone and easy flow'.

Special attention is paid to *The Watsons*: it is 'untypical in being focussed on a semi-genteel family that suffers from straitened income and its frequent accompaniments of drabness and meanness of life and outlook'. Bush emphasizes that it reads like a play because of the incidence of dialogue, which is revelatory of character. *Sense and Sensibility* provides illustrations of the maturity and immaturity of Jane Austen's technical ability: Bush finds the story 'nearer tragedy than comedy and it has more sharp satire than humour'. He says that her 'style is a more or less subtle index or reflection of moral and cultural differences'.

The opening of *Pride and Prejudice*, so often regarded with uncritical affection, is here closely scrutinized: 'In a way characteristic of a stylist of ironic nuances, the mock-philosophical solemnity of the first clause is immediately deflated by a notion of marriage appropriate to high comedy'. Later Bush notes that proposals reported directly through dialogue in a Jane Austen novel are those which are rejected. This seems to be evidence of the comic perspective. He also asserts Jane Austen's sense of structure in this novel quite beautifully – 'And economy contributes much to the graceful, coherent symmetry'. The 'main vehicle' of the book is dialogue, which here subserves characterization, comedy and satire.

Mansfield Park is also about marriage like all Jane Austen's novels, exposing 'with deadpan irony the commercial view' of it obtained in her world. The movement here is away from simple hero–heroine narrative to groups of people and their interrelationships. The central incident – the theatricals – 'is clearly a signal example of the moral urgency that distinguishes *Mansfield Park* as a whole'. The central issue, however, is 'decorum': it is also the book 'in which Jane

Austen conducted her deepest explorations of the human heart and head'. The techniques of *Emma* reflect the complexity of that masterpiece. Bush divides the novel into episodes, the Elton one, for example, 'so handled as to initiate readers into the ironic method'. In the final measure he finds *Emma* 'a completely realistic, consistent, and searching novel of character and personal relations.... *Emma* is, especially through its sustained irony, a masterpiece of development, or organic unity of form and tone'.

Persuasion is neatly summarized (a quality of Bush's book is a tendency to précis situations), as is *Sanditon*: among other conclusions it seems to me that Bush's selection of her 'instinct for order and proportion' being both 'ethical and artistic', the two strains being 'complementary and inseparable', is correct. This is a fitting volume for the time, evaluating achievement and indicating the main qualities and, if not new, it is consummately balanced, as sane and responsible as its subject.

Marilyn Butler's *Jane Austen and the War of Ideas* (1975; new introduction 1987) is a major study of Jane Austen and her attitudes. Although it has provoked measures of disagreement, there can be no denying its importance or the strength of its arguments. As she says, the novels of Jane Austen and her contemporaries 'were full of signs which conveyed opinions'. She feels that Jane Austen was part of 'a conservative reaction' against the freer novels which preceded hers.

I have referred to the new introduction above since Marilyn Butler indicates that the reissue of her book 'places it in a discussion dominated by feminism'. Having particularized the nature of feminist bias in some recent criticism, she asserts – and it seems to me that her standpoint here is an enlightened one – that 'To read a Jane Austen novel as *only* a woman's novel, is, then, to read it selectively. But not to read it as *among other things* a woman's novel is also, as feminist criticism has taught all of us, to leave a proper historical dimension out'. The study is punctuated by astute comments, such as the one in whch she observes almost casually that in the late works Jane Austen increasingly

appears to be 'a social commentator'. Miss Butler uses 'particularized historical criticism', her aim being to 'reconstruct
the context in which women writers wrote', while 'seeing
their culture whole will also mean daring to see it diverse,
fragmented and contested, not dubiously simplified for prop-
agandist or teaching purposes'. This needs to be said, since
so much that is written about Jane Austen smacks of self-indulgence.

Miss Butler continues unequivocal in emphasis, firmly
assertive whether she is dealing with Jane Austen's detail
('She skewers a moral solecism as confidently as a verbal
infelicity') or total effect ('the very last impression left by an
Austen novel is one of doubt'). Nor does Miss Butler have any
doubts: 'Jane Austen's novels belong decisively to one class
of partisan novels, the conservative.... Her important innovations are technical'. The aim, therefore, is to place Jane
Austen firmly in her context, in her genre, and to attempt 'to
define her meaning, and, in the process, to isolate what is
unique in her work, its ultimate originality'.

The background of sentimentalism and its connections is
thoroughly delved, through the 18th-century novel, with the
dominance of the hero, and a particular examination of
Mackenzie's *Julia de Roubigne* (1777), in the chapter 'Sentimentalism: The Radical Inheritance'. This sentimental love-
story revolves around a young girl's choice of a marriage
partner (certainly a Jane Austen theme), but 'The radical
nature of the representation is underlined by the fact that
the truly "pure" passion in the novel is extra-marital'. The
continuing examination of the Jacobin novel takes in Mrs
Radcliffe, while Bage's *Hermsprong* (1796) was certainly in
Jane Austen's possession. Miss Butler observes 'Bage's entire
novel sets out to do what is done only by certain scenes and
characters in *Pride and Prejudice* – to deflate the swollen
pride of the representatives of the State and the Church'.
Additionally, Bage lays 'his emphasis on dialogue as an index
of value'. There are some telling observations in the chapter
on 'The Anti-Jacobins', for example, 'In discussing the use
made of *Lovers' Vows* in *Mansfield Park* (1814) modern com-
mentators sometimes underrate how notorious it was; how

critics and satirists from *The Anti-Jacobin* on had made it a byword for moral and social subversion'. Miss Butler's sideways glances are always effective, for instance, in her judgement that 'in feeling for the social virtues of the country as opposed to the selfish virtues of the town... Jane West anticipates Jane Austen', and also that like Jane Austen's heroines, hers learn that 'objective evidence should be preferred to private intuition'.

Northanger Abbey and *Sense and Sensibility* 'display broadly the typical attitudes of the feminine type of conservative novel'. She notes, however, that in *Lady Susan* 'she does attempt a villain, a cruising shark in her social goldfish pond', though 'In the conservative novel, society itself is the real hero'. Next, she turns to the important influence of Maria Edgeworth who, she believes, deliberately fashioned the kind of novel which would be 'especially relevant to women readers'. Miss Butler also believes that her social comedy (in *Belinda* for instance) 'must surely have made a contribution to Jane Austen's, where values are also revealed through contrasting a whole range of characters and deploying in the comparison every nuance of speech'. The choice of language here can only underline the strength of the point, and there follows a superb analysis of the relevance of *Leonora*.

Part II of this study focusses in detail on Jane Austen, her practices and attitudes. She feels that 'her manner as a novelist is broadly that of the conservative Christian moralist of the 1790's', her 'lineaments' being those of 'the committed conservative'. The analyses of the *Juvenilia* and *Northanger Abbey* include the recognition that Jane Austen was slow to develop the inner life, as compared with her confident handling of dialogue, but Miss Butler's conclusion, superbly put, indicates the nature of Jane Austen's overall achievement in the novel – 'the feat of the subtlest technician among the English novelists, is to re-think the material of the conservative novel in terms that are at once naturalistic and intellectually consistent'. It is a large claim finely argued and more than partly demonstrated: we may disagree with some of the emphases or conclusions, but the sweep of the analysis forces us, I suggest, to re-think too: we should regard that as one of the functions of good criticism.

Sense and Sensibility 'is unremittingly didactic', for 'The entire action is organized to represent Elinor and Marianne in terms of rival value-systems'. She observes that Marianne 'and our responses to her, are outside Jane Austen's control', an indication of our sympathy for her despite what we may be asked to feel. The look at *Pride and Prejudice* questions whether it runs counter to the conservative theme, since it has so often been highly rated 'on account of its supposedly radical' one. Miss Butler does not accept this, though she acknowledges that 'in lacking clarity it is untypical'.

The close examination of *Mansfield Park* is preceded by the statement that it is 'the most imaginative and accomplished of received anti-Jacobin novels'. There are interesting comments on the structure, where a form of triple contrast is employed in terms of education and moral attitude, the three being common to most scenes. The ideology of the novel can be deduced from the visit to Sotherton, but the difficulties in *Mansfield Park* are associated with the presentation of Fanny. Her lack of force is an attempt to make her appealing (more human when set beside some of the other characters). She goes so far as to feel that Fanny is a failure. If much of this is self-evident, the chapter on *Emma* is crisp and sharp. She notes the vitality of this novel, and says that the theme covers the attempt to reach 'a fixed and permanent truth' which is outside the individual existence. This, of necessity, is 'chastening' to the self-hood 'presumption' of the individual. I must agree with this, and the appraisal of Miss Bates and Mr Woodhouse leads her to the conclusion that the inherent comic qualities of each is also revelatory of moral incapacity. *Persuasion* clumsily combines new and old modes, but *Sanditon* strikingly illustrates how intellectually consistent her writing has been throughout – the experiment may be subjective but the philosophy which informs it is unchanged. Miss Butler has come back to her starting point and to Jane Austen's: in my end is my beginning, for all six of the novels are inherently conservative and so they remain. This is reinforced by the fact that the important sequences in the novels represent conservative attitudes 'in an active war of ideas'. More controversial is the assertion that Jane Austen is not 'natural', that she censors the inner lives of her creatures. I suspect for most readers this would amount to a natural selectivity, although it is difficult not to agree with Miss Butler when she instances the sensuous, the irrational, the 'involuntary types of mental experience' as being disapproved of by Jane Austen. It seems to me that this demonstrates that Jane Austen is conditioned by her time. Miss Butler finds her morality pre-conditioned and set, and thus the buttress of her conservatism: Miss Butler's study is both provocative and stimulating, brilliantly incisive and admirably clear in its main direction.

Barbara Hardy's *A Reading of Jane Austen* (1975; reprinted 1979) is finely and sensitively conceived and unequivocally direct. The first statement is indicative of the quality we shall find throughout: 'Good artists work within their chosen genre, great artists transform it'. It is the kind of definitive conception which categorizes the unique greatness of Jane Austen. Mrs Hardy tells us that 'The flexible medium is the dominant gift of her genius' and this is seen, for instance, in the way that 'She applies a very gentle pressure to bring out the minute but real problems of social life'. Macaulay found an analogy with Shakespeare, and Mrs Hardy provides her own with insightful particularity: 'The subtexts of social occasion were not invented by Jane Austen, but she makes a fuller and more subtle use of them than anyone since Shakespeare'. The reader can demonstrate the accuracy of this statement by recourse to any number of the fictional gatherings.

The 'natural' quality of Jane Austen's approach is stressed, for 'she moves lightly and unobtrusively from character to group, close-up to distance'. This flexibility, one feels, is art concealing art, and, I feel inclined to add, that it is purposefully integrated into the flow of narrative.

'The Feelings and the Passions' are investigated with sympathetic insistence, and 'In all the novels the stream of feeling is sufficiently marked in its private moments for us to be aware of its constant motion beneath the formal social

surfaces'. Another phrase – 'the underground strength of
feeling' – is part of the reader's awareness and response to
'the revelations of inner action, the moments of feeling un-
bared in privacy and solitude and silence'. The structures
have an inherent balance, for 'The successive waves of feeling
and reflection on feeling are characteristic of Jane Austen
and utterly central in each novel'. This is more than probing:
it is definitive of head and heart art, and we are inclined to
agree when Mrs Hardy asserts that 'Jane Austen is not an
extroverted social novelist, interested chiefly in the series of
external impressions, but conceives her heroines as imaginative beings, able to accomodate their responses to the movements of the larger world'.

Each novel 'has its flow of telling and listening'. A typical
Hardy triplet evaluates 'Continuity, Climax and Conclusion',
and here there is a fine section on the weaving of internal
narrative, 'the private crisis of feeling'. She notes the incidence in each novel of the piece of 'transforming news' as
well as the listening reactions to story, which are often of
astonishment. There is the repeated situation at the end of
a Jane Austen novel, or at least in its final section, which
admits of 'confidence, confessions, blurted-out secrets, tran-
sient attempts to deceive'. In the second section on the
storytellers, Mrs Hardy notes that in Jane Austen 'telling
and listening...is an analysis and an evaluation of the human
mind'. One feels that this is a further indication of Jane
Austen's narrative subtlety, her in-depth contemplation of
individuals in their convincing fictional lives. The process is
one of development: 'The heroines all have to learn the right
use of imaginative energy, to direct it towards the self and
towards the world', and here she concludes that 'What the
critic laboriously analyses, the novelist knows'. The emphasis is right – it is the ultimate recognition of conscious
art. There is some perceptive comment on the 'Social Groups'
present in each Jane Austen novel: Mrs Hardy observes that
'The bounds of her coteries and groups are constantly broken,
and their closeness challenged, by fresh arrivals and departures'. This structural constant is reinforced by the fact that
'Her moral analysis of character is also conducted in her

group dramas'. We might then say that her subtlety consists of having a number of fictional balls in the air at the same time, with complete control of the movement and final resting place of each. One of the famous set pieces of *Emma* is seen in this way: 'Through ritual, structure, and character, the Box Hill picnic is attached to the novel's past, which has been intent on the festivities and games played in groups'. Some groups, she says, are 'controlled or dominated by leaders', while the social gatherings are 'analytic and comic' and linked 'smoothly and tensely' – this seeming paradox defining Jane Austen's method and her practice.

There is an original section on 'Properties and Possessions' which 'begin to be fully animated in *Northanger Abbey*'. This aspect of Jane Austen's art has always needed fuller definition I feel, and here there is orchestration. Mrs Hardy records the symbolic effects of the house and its contents. She stresses Jane Austen's 'knowledge of her characters' attitudes to houses, clothes and accessories' and how that 'extends to other creature comforts'. In *Emma* 'hospitality and donation become prominent themes'. Mrs Hardy's 'Sense of the Author' underlines, I think, the profound sense of her enlightened evaluation:

> Her rule in the mature novels is to charm and amuse by powers of wit, imagination and satire, but at the same time to assimilate the wits, critics, and satirists into the moral action and subject them most severely to critical judgement. Wit, imagination and satire are set free, suspected, tried and found wanting.

Joan Rees' *Jane Austen: Woman and Writer* (1976) uses much quotation from the *Letters* since the author wishes her subject to 'speak for herself as much as possible'. The first section of this study covers ground already much explored by other writers (though deeper exploration was undertaken in the 1980s), with its emphasis on the part played by Jane Austen's family in her development. Miss Rees records that very few of the surviving letters were addressed to people outside Jane Austen's immediate circle. This is followed by a perceptive survey of family-based biography and a brief factual account of her life, in the process of which Miss Rees utters some independent asides such as 'Nevertheless Jane Austen was to grow up without any undue reverence for the clergy'. One has only to think passingly of Mr Elton, for example, or perhaps more probingly of Mr Collins to underline the truth of this observation.

There is a competent summary of the *Juvenilia*, with the assertion that *Catherine* offers the clearest prophecy of the riches to come. Here, Miss Rees considers the style and characterization, particularly of what she feels is the development from caricature, together with the emergence of Jane Austen's highly 'individual tone of voice', as well as the recognizable themes of her maturity. Like other critics before and after her, she indicates the unique, or at least the unexpected, conception of the character of Lady Susan. Miss Rees shows some subtlety here in clearly categorizing the varied nature of the presentation. For the reader unfamiliar with the *Juvenilia* this is an admirable, succinct and critically aware introduction.

The second chapter is an investigation of the position of women and more directly the status of women writers in Jane Austen's time. Miss Rees contends that Jane Austen always wrote with the ambition of having her work published, and that therefore, by the standards of that time, she was already 'an emancipated woman'. She alludes to the common attack on Jane Austen's limitations – that she only wrote about the middle-class, and that the major events of her time did not impinge upon her work – but she considers that these supposed limitations, and Jane Austen's own recognition of them, were in fact evidence of her own particularized strength. Later, critics were to probe more fully the fact that the novels were not as limited as they might appear to be, and Miss Rees argues convincingly that the author's prescribed focus allows her to establish 'an innate core of reality' which would have been undermined by the introduction 'of characters or events drawn without knowledge or experience'. Miss Rees herself is drawn to biography and speculation, and this sometimes runs counter to her obviously detailed knowledge of the novels. The main direction of her tracings is also obvious, from the impact of Thomas Lefroy to Jane as housekeeper through the Leigh Perrot case to the departure from Steventon. Chapter Three follows the chronological pattern, though there is an interesting section which suggests that during Jane Austen's supposedly fallow period she was, in fact, much occupied with an early draft of *Mansfield Park*: this theory posits that it belongs in 1808-9 (an idea already put forward by Q.D. Leavis), since 'the chronology is based on the calendars of 1808 and 1809'. Miss Rees goes on to instance correspondences between Jane's life and events in the novel, referring to the views of her cousin Eliza – married to Jane's brother Henry – on ordination, and connects these with Mary Crawford's avowed distaste for Edmund's coming profession. Jane visited Stoneleigh Abbey during the summer of 1808, which perhaps contributed to the descriptions of Sotherton. Miss Rees further suggests that the 'formidible aunt', Mrs Leigh Perrot, could have influenced the conception of the most unpleasant aunt in Jane Austen's fiction, Mrs Norris.

Jane also refers to the game of speculation at this time, a game used as a discriminating index to character in *Mansfield Park*. Miss Rees also suggests that Jane's account to Cassandra of the 'runaway Mrs Powlett'(*Letters* 197, 20 June 1808), may have provided the germ for the sensational plot-convenient elopement of Maria and Henry Crawford in the novel.

Chapter Four of Miss Rees' study is appropriately entitled 'The Years of Fulfilment'; it continues with the biographical emphasis which marks her method, generally perceptive, often particularized, as in 'If the figure of Cassandra remains somewhat shadowy, it is largely because she features in the correspondence as the participant in a dialogue who never replies'. If the life teases by virtue of what we cannot know with certainty, however, the fiction provides the compensatory fulfilment with the publication of *Sense and Sensibility* in 1811. It moves Miss Rees to direct critical appraisal. She refuses to accept the simplistic definition of the novels as 'social comedies', choosing to concur instead with Malcolm

Bradbury's assertion that they are 'moral assault courses...
in which the candidates give their qualifications, undergo a
succession of tests, and are finally rewarded by the one prize
that is possible and appropriate in their social context –
marriage' (*Emma: A Casebook*, ed. D. Lodge, p. 218). In her
probing of *Sense and Sensibility* Miss Rees pertinently asks
'between whom were the letters written?' We recall that
Elinor and Marianne, the original title of *Sense and Sensibility*, was supposedly in the 18th-century epistolary form.
Miss Rees shrewdly notes that the correspondence could
hardly have between Elinor and Marianne, since the writers
'were never apart'. But perhaps we should observe that, as
in all Jane Austen's novels, there are some telling letters in
Sense and Sensibility, for example, Marianne's letter to Willoughby and the latter's wife-dictated letter to her. We can
see that the movement of the plot – and the movement of
location – would also be conducive to the epistolary structure.
    Miss Rees sees *Pride and Prejudice* 'as a duel between the
hero and the heroine', while she finds the presentation of
Charlotte Lucas 'unique' and of especial interest. Perhaps
predictably she connects Darcy with Heathcliff and Roches-
ter because of his 'dramatic physical presence'. Always alert
to the biographical association, Miss Rees feels that one of
the visitors to Godmersham, Mrs Britton, may well have
provided the outline for Mrs Elton in *Emma*, for Jane describes her in a letter as a 'large, ungenteel woman, with
self-satisfied and would-be elegant manners'. Miss Rees also
finds the response of Jane's niece Anna to Fanny Price (whom
she could not stand), anticipatory of certain modern responses, for example, that of Kingsley Amis ('the character
of Fanny lacks self-knowledge, generosity and humility') or
Marvin Mudrick, who calls her 'a frozen block of timidity'. In
her own analysis of *Mansfield Park*, Miss Rees finds that the
'Portsmouth sequence is done with Dickensian realism'.
Again there is some shrewd evaluation of Jane Austen's
reiterative concerns and their variety, as in the observation
that the heroines of the novels are brought through experience to a full self-knowledge, whereas in *Mansfield Park*, it
is 'the middle-aged man of substance and dignity, Sir Thomas

Bertram' who is brought to a new appraisal of himself, his life and his limitations. Interesting too is Miss Rees' focus on the character of Emma, who mirrors her creator, she feels, in her occasional 'inability to control her tongue', as in the celebrated incident with Miss Bates. There is certainly evidence in Jane Austen's letters to support Miss Rees here, though perhaps we should be cautious about the claim that 'through Emma, Jane Austen was also blaming and absolving herself'. Miss Rees also claims that Frank Churchill lacks the complexity of previous characters of the same type as Wickham, Willoughby and Henry Crawford, which seems dubious. It is surely the ironic perspective which is different in quality here.

The last year or so of Jane Austen's life is pertinently summarized, and there is some useful commentary on *Sanditon*, where again the biographical link is made, with Jane Austen's exquisite sense of humour remaining with her to the end. Miss Rees believes that her mother's 'hypochondria', which her daughter had put up with for many years, almost certainly influenced the broad comic treatment found in *Sanditon* (and of course earlier in the presentation of Mr Woodhouse). The final pages of this book are devoted to *Northanger Abbey* and *Persuasion*, together with some speculation about Jane Austen's attitude towards death. She concludes that basically Jane Austen was an optimist, and mentions the word 'charm' in association with her four times on the last half page of her study. If Miss Rees' critical commentary is mainly low-key, her linking of the biographical with the fictional is often perceptive, while the summary of Jane Austen's achievements and concerns is neatly, warmly but not cloyingly put. It is a fitting, discriminating and sensitive centenary tribute.

Lord David Cecil's *A Portrait of Jane Austen* (1978) builds a bridge, I believe, between the Janeites and serious criticism and scholarship. The Foreword is sufficiently modest, with Cecil claiming that the book is 'an attempt, with the help of material drawn from her letters, her novels and other people's memories of her, to reconstruct and depict her living personality and explore her relation to her art'. In fact, the book depicts through pictorial accompaniment to commentary, the visual foreground and background of her time, so that its coffee-table location is never in doubt. He claims that she 'was the very voice and typical representative of her world' (whatever world that may be) and adds 'my views of Jane Austen's art have changed little since 1935'. This shows, and in the light of modern criticism and biography, irks by the confined nature of its tone, a preservationist rather than a probing manner. Cecil asserts 'Her novels were not personal revelations' (all great novels, I think, are 'personal' and 'revelations' in a sense), though he adduces from her letters, which have a 'sharp, subtle, agreeable flavour' that she was 'perhaps formidable'. There is a suitable summary of the culture, morality and social realism of the 18th century, which 'succeeded in combining good sense, good manners and cultivated intelligence, rational piety and a spirited sense of fun. Certainly it suited Jane Austen'. The statement can hardly be regarded as blandly definitive, as modern investigations, or at least a fair proportion of them, have been at pains to demonstrate.

There follows a reasoned and reasonable account of the Austen family and culture, what Cecil says here in small and elegant compass having since been more fully explored and reinvigorated by Park Honan (see pp. 118-24). There is also sound evaluation of her early works: 'We learn from them that she was a precocious genius, in her style, in her power of observation, in her characteristic vein of humour'. The blandness, however, predominates, as in 'The mental climate in which she grew up enabled her genius to develop unhampered, undistracted, unforced'. We know from the letters, however, that often something more powerful than a ripple disturbed the stream. There are interesting suggestions, for example, in Cecil's examination of her attitude to the death of Sir John Moore, who, she thought, put his country before God on his death-bed.

Jane Austen inevitably attracts psychological approaches in our own time. One of these is Bernard J. Paris' *Character and Conflict in Jane Austen's Novels: A Psychological Approach* (1978), in which the author asserts that Jane Austen's characters have to be understood 'in motivational terms'. He employs the theories of Northrop Frye to analyse the comic structures of the novels, and Karen Horney's psychological theories 'to analyse her characters and her authorial personality'. He believes that Jane Austen's personality is 'a structure of inner conflicts', but that she is 'a great comic artist, a serious interpreter of life, and a creator of brilliant mimetic characterisations'. There is little to disagree with in this last statement, but some emphases do not allow a free response. For example, we might agree that 'She harmonises form and theme by moralising the comic action', since the emphasis shows how aware of her art Jane Austen is, but I think we would query a statement such as 'In order to appreciate Jane Austen's true genius in characterisation, we must approach her major figures as creations inside a creation and try to understand them as though they were real people'. This is the basic premise of the book, ironically placing the author closer to the Janeites than to his professional practice. Yet so rich is Jane Austen's literary personality (and personalities) that we can see the value of the approach, particularly when he says that 'Manners change and values are debateable, but human needs and conflicts remain much the same, and mimetic truth endures'. This is perhaps the reason for Jane Austen's comprehensive transcendence of her own time and her compulsive interest for ours.

Paris' concentration on *Mansfield Park* means a close examination of Fanny Price. He believes that his method of analysis will show 'a rather different Fanny from the one the author thinks she has portrayed'. Some ground covered here has been covered elsewhere, as in his belief that 'We do not sympathise with Fanny as much or find her as interesting as we might because Austen asks us to admire her'. Paris suggests, however, that Fanny is 'a complex and fascinating psychological portrait'. He stresses that although she comes to physical maturity, she remains a young child psychologically. I believe it is far more likely that she becomes a heavily conditioned adult. Paris is critical of the ending of the novel, finding it 'not true to experience' and 'an indulgence of the heroine'.

Further divisions and inconsistencies occur in *Emma*. Paris states that the heroine is 'an imagined human being whose personal qualities are not always in harmony with her dramatic and thematic functions'. The implication, as in *Mansfield Park*, is that there are divisions between Jane Austen's intentions and our contemplation of her end-product: 'It is quite possible, it seems to me, both to experience *Emma* from Jane Austen's point of view, to know what she thinks she is doing, and to recognise that the novel which she has actually created does not always support her intentions.' There is a set arrogance about this which I find difficult to accept: the extra dimensions which come from the unconscious or subconscious (or intuition) seem to me to be an index to genius. Paris goes on to argue strongly and well (having indicated her 'narcissistic and perfectionist trends') that Emma is basically insecure, that she is in competition with Mrs Elton, and that her 'scheming should be seen as, in part at least, an expression of her need for reassurance'. He also notes that she is too resilient to be put off by failure. There is a subtle notation of her relationship with her father; Paris feels that she represses her irritation with him, but that her feelings are 'displaced onto Miss Bates', an ingenious theory and quite possible.

This full contemplation leads to a comparative evaluation. The suggestion here is that Emma and Fanny Price are mainly 'opposite psychological types', and Paris rightly finds it a major achievement on Jane Austen's part that she could reveal the inner lives of such largely different characters. Paris astutely observes that *Pride and Prejudice* is concerned as much with 'manners as with "marriage" ', while he finds *Persuasion* combines seriousness and romance, again something we would not dispute. He defines Anne Elliot's motivation with the successful internalizing of her standards which derive from her determined need for self-approval. A comparison is made between Anne and Fanny, the curve of the narrative bringing each from apparent failure to eventual triumph. This seems to me a limited reading.

The 'perfectionist' emphasis is applied to the author's personality via Horneyan psychology. Her code of values is asserted, and this includes her fascination with 'the cult of sensibility'. For Jane Austen, an excess of worldliness violates the code (a good example of the extreme is Lady Susan); Paris also notes the sense of detachment in her writing, with values and virtues of self-control, privacy and endurance.

Patrick Piggott's *The Innocent Diversion: A Study of Music in the Life and Writings of Jane Austen* (1979) fills another gap in the foreground and background. Piggott points out the importance of music in the social life of the times, and in her novels the heroines (and anti-heroines) play an instrument, with the exception of Catherine Morland, while Jane Fairfax performs superbly on the pianoforte. But Jane Austen seems to have had an ambivalent attitude towards listening to music. Her stay in Bath (1801-6) would have afforded her plenty of opportunity to attend concerts. In her letters to Cassandra she sometimes mentions a concert, commenting not on the music, but on what she wore. Yet a few months before her death she wrote to her niece Caroline 'The Piano-Forte often talks of you; – in various keys, tunes and 'expressions I allow – but be it lesson or Country Dance, Sonata or Waltz, *you* are really its constant Theme' (*Letters* 473).

Piggott examines the *Minor Works* and sees anticipations of *Sense and Sensibility* in *Lesley Castle*, with 'the two sister heroines of contrasting temperaments, one of them musical'. *Lady Susan* provides evidence of musical attainments 'in young girls about to be thrown on the marriage market'. Marianne plays and sings very well, and part of Willoughby's specious appeal is his ability to copy out music. As she grieves for him, Marianne resorts more and more to her music, as the index to her suffering: which is 'a symbol for Marianne Dashwood's extravagant emotionalism'. In *Pride and Prejudice* we find that music is used to underline sensitivity and limitation, for Mary plays well but chooses unsuitable music, and continues to play beyond reason. Later she offends by her affectation – 'her voice was weak, and her manner affected. Elizabeth was in agonies'. There is an ironic glance at Lady Catherine's interest in music, despite the fact that she has never learned to play.

Mary Crawford's harp is part of the symbolic structure of

Mansfield Park. The emphasis is interesting: 'for she played with the greatest obligingness, with an expression which was peculiarly becoming, and there was something clever to be said at the close of every air'. Music draws Edmund to Mary and away from Fanny, and Mary herself feels threatened by 'the possible musical accomplishments of the Miss Owens', who may in turn draw Edmund away from her. There are 'varied uses for music' in *Emma*, and as an important plot pivot there is the arrival of the pianoforte for Jane Fairfax at Miss Bates' home. Emma plays and sings a little and without distinction, for she starts up many interests and finishes none. Naturally she is seen in competition with Jane Fairfax, while Frank Churchill's references to Jane playing music are used to conceal his real interest in her. Another significant moment occurs when 'Jane's voice is showing signs of fatigue', and Knightley becomes angry with Frank Churchill, who is urging her to continue. Again a moral index is made evident by Jane Austen.

In *Persuasion* the scene of the public concert in the New Assembly Rooms is another plot pivot. Piggott virtually establishes the date as 22nd February 1815, when Anne and Captain Wentworth meet at the concert, the *Bath Chronicle* confirming the performance of the time. Next, Piggott turns to the Chawton collection of Jane Austen's music books. There are two books of major importance, 'one of songs written throughout in her own hand' but she appears to have lacked what she would have called 'taste' as regards her choice of songs and piano pieces. There is a second collection which contains works by Cramer, the only composer named in her works (*Emma*). Piggott feels that all this leads to the conclusion that 'Jane Austen was certainly more musical than she sometimes chose to allow'.

8

Feminist and Other Criticism and Biography in the 1980s: A Selection

Margaret Kirkham, in *Jane Austen, Feminism and Fiction* (1983) is often found to be in opposition to the views and interpretations of Marilyn Butler. Her context is that of 'eighteenth century feminist ideas and the Feminist Controversy of the turn of the eighteenth century'. Jane Austen's stance, she says, is 'indicative of her sympathy with the rational feminism of the Enlightenment', with 'her central moral interest in the moral nature of woman and her *role* in society'. Consequently she sets out 'to relate Austen as literary artist and innovator to her declared position as feminist moralist and critic of fictional tradition', for she has 'the feminist insistence, in her day, upon women as "rational creatures" ', demonstrating 'their artistic competence in the new literary form'.

The section on 'Feminism and Fiction' is a fascinating prelude, since Miss Kirkham maintains that the emergence of female authors encouraged the development of feminism, with a certain amount of apprehension. The fear lay largely in the fact that impressionable readers would be adversely influenced. In dealing with *Sir Charles Grandison* and the overall effects of the repeated readings on Jane Austen, she concludes that she had a distinctly critical view of it 'and some antipathy to Richardson in general'. She feels that the morality was questionable, and mocked Harriet Byron. Furthermore, Miss Kirkham feels that Jane Austen's anti-Romanticism 'is an aspect of her feminism', adding 'In her own novels, Austen criticizes the belief that woman's problems are to be solved by benevolent patriarchs'. I feel inclined to add that they are also created by unbenevolent patriarchs too.

She indicates the influence of *A Vindication of the Rights of Women* (1792), with 'its emphasis upon the authority of Reason and rational principle as the only true guide to right conduct'. Rousseau's influence here is stressed, though his attitude towards the education of women was that it 'should be always relative to men'. Miss Kirkham devalues the *Biographical Notice*, suggesting that it should be more accurately titled the 'Hagiographical Notice'. She moves on to the defence of the novel as a literary form in *Northanger Abbey*, remarking on its strength 'and the idea given of its scope and importance'. She describes Jane Austen's scepticism about 'History' as feminist, adding that here 'she anticipates a later age'. She also finds Jane Austen's response to Scott's review of *Emma* feminist in its sarcasm at his omission of *Mansfield Park* from the notice.

Most interesting is the critical focus on the early novels in which she explores Jane Austen's comic vision. She suggests that she enlarges the range of comic perspective by giving it a serious intention – embodying criticism of manners, morals and certainly of current literature. The heroines are not self-conscious feminists but they endorse the idea that women ought to have the same 'moral status' as men since they have the same nature, and they should also be responsible for their own conduct.

There are similar provocative assertions to come. Miss Kirkham contends that the later novels contain criticisms of 'law, manners and customs' because they do not treat women as they are, but as it is felt they ought to be. Next she points out that *Mansfield Park* and *Emma* are rooted in theatrical allusion, with Kotzebue (author of the translated *Lover's Vows*) as the irritant who moves Jane Austen to major achievement. He is, of course, inferior to Shakespeare, who created women with 'mixed characters'. She contrasts Fanny in *Mansfield Park* with Sophie in *Émile*, and also shows how Fanny overcomes the feeble ideal she seems to represent. Of greater interest, one feels, is the idea that *Mansfield Park* in its three-volume structure approximates to the three-act play. This is followed by a historical glance at the Mansfield Judgement, which made slavery in England illegal. She adds that Sir Thomas is a slave-owner abroad and his wife is virtually enslaved in England, the analogy between slaves and married women in England having been already traced by Mary Wollstonecraft in the *Vindication*. Furthermore, *Mansfield Park* apparently embodies ideas of liberty, equality and fraternity with a feminist emphasis. Kotzebue also figures as an influence on *Emma*. In his play *The Birthday*, and in Jane Austen's novel, the heroines are constrained not to marry because they each have sick fathers to care for. Brief references to the play support this, while in Eaton Stannard Barrett's *The Heroine* (1813; read by Jane Austen in 1814) Cherubina (Cherry) is a mischief-maker in the love affairs of village girls. Miss Kirkham says Jane Austen enjoyed and used this 'burlesque stereotype, as well as mocking romantic delusions'. She feels that Jane Austen's 'feminist viewpoint', corrects Barrett's presentation of these particular stereotypes in the shape of the governess, the natural imbecility of young women, illegitimacy and the hero as mentor. The direct connection of these with *Emma* will be apparent. We see the sharpness of Miss Kirkham's eye in her appraisal of a list of names deriving from Jane Austen's first season in Bath in 1801-2, which stuck in her mind and were fed into various of the novels ('Sir John and Lady Knightley', 'Dr. Campbell and Mr Coles', 'Sir John and Lady Palmer', and an obituary of the actress 'Mrs Crawford' are examples).

Persuasion and *Sanditon* support Miss Kirkham's thesis: Anne's conversation with Captain Harville 'puts a feminist point of view' in 'men have had every advantage of us in telling their own story. Education has been theirs in so much higher a degree; the pen has been in their hands'. Anne is distinctly, and more than the other heroines, 'the central moral intelligence of the novel'. In *Sanditon*, Sir Edward Denham constitutes 'her most outright attack on Richardson'. Miss Kirkham's book is convincingly argued and clearly emphatic, constantly engaging the reader's sympathies and intellect.

The Foreword to George Holbert Tucker's *A Goodly Heritage: A History of Jane Austen's Family* (1983) refers to the study as being of 'precise, careful scholarship', and the Preface stresses the fact that Jane Austen is not the centre of the book. It is suggested that she would have appreciated this, since she was remarkably modest and acknowledged the importance of her family in her writing. It is Tucker's contention that she received inestimable benefits from being 'an outstanding example of the social class that she depicted so discerningly – the landed gentry of England'. He traces her paternal ancestry back to the reign of Elizabeth I; farming, weaving and considerable possession of property accrued. Property and preferment came the way of the Reverend George Austen, Jane's father, a man noteworthy for his discrimination and culture. As we know, he was a good classicist, and his holding of the modest livings of Staunton and Deane is a measure of the fact that he was not interested in pursuing material gain to the exclusion of spiritual and cultivated welfare. Tucker draws attention to Henry's mention of him in the biographical notice to *Northanger Abbey* and *Persuasion*, where he said that he was 'not only a profound scholar, but possessing a most exquisite taste in every species of literature'. His tolerance and gentleness of nature are reflected in the fact that he did not pursue any of his parishoners who didn't pay their tithes. Some insight into his life at Tonbridge is given, followed by a brief sketch of his time at St John's College, Oxford. From 1754-7 he was both perpetual curate at Shipbourne, Kent, as well as an usher at Tonbridge. He returned to St John's and was ordained in 1760. He was then presented to the living of Staunton in 1761 through the patronage of Thomas Knight of Godmersham, his cousin, though he did not take up his duties until 1764. In April of that year he married Cassandra Leigh. The Austens stayed at Deane until 1768, when the 'refurbished rectory at Steventon' was ready for them. They lived there until George Austen retired and they re-moved to Bath in 1801. As rector of Deane, George Austen had enjoyed a comfortable livelihood and a high social status, and in addition to his two holdings, he supplemented his income by farming and taking private pupils. These details and others support Tucker's belief that the Austens 'created a contented world and happy home atmosphere conducive to character development'. Most important is the fact that George Austen was most certainly a great reader of novels: his interest in his daughter's fiction is, of course, well documented.

Tucker gives, for the first time, the correct transcription of his letter to Cadell of 1st November 1797 concerning *First Impressions*, and asserts that 'his real distinction was an early and appreciative perception of Jane Austen's literary gifts'. After the Hancock—Hastings survey, Tucker spends some time looking at the aristocratic Leigh family, who existed on a rather higher social plane 'than the somewhat staid Austens of Kent'. One of the Leigh ancestors, Sir Thomas, achieved high office in civil life, and the 'Leigh cup' which he left to the Mercers' Company is still used. The ancestry on this side is traced right through to Dr Theophilus Leigh (1693-1785), who was Master of Balliol for more than fifty years. His 'dubious puns and scholarly jests' were appreciated by generations of Austens. Tucker refers to Thomas Leigh, the youngest brother of Jane's mother, who was brought up outside the family presumably because he was mentally retarded. Tucker devotes much space to Mrs Austen, and this I feel is one of the most positive aspects of his study, which seeks to show how strongly the various aspects of family inheritance and life affected the novelist. She received, in the broad term, culture, from her father, particularized in disciplined and discriminating reading and judgement, an ability to be rational, and a feeling for words always evident in her developing style. But Tucker stresses that 'From her clever mother she derived lively wit, ironic humour, and an accurate perception of character'. J.E. Austen-Leigh had already referred to her 'epigrammatic force and point'. Tucker believes that she provided important aspects of Jane Austen's education, citing as evidence a finished and delightfully expressed letter which reflects the quality of her mind. Here Tucker is breaking new ground. There are many testimonies to her domestic talents, especially her neat and even dedication to managing the Rectory at Steventon (witness Anna Lefroy and J.E. Austen-Leigh). She was a forthright woman, with a delightful sense of humour, seen in some doggerel verses written in reaction to the Rectory being crowded by her husband's pupils. It was not until the 1790s that she became something of a hypochondriac, and it is while the family is living at Sydney Place, Bath, that she has a serious illness. Tucker quotes, in support of her sense of fun, a fine piece of doggerel about death coming for her, but I find genuine pathos in her explanation that she owes her survival to the doctor, and 'To the prayers of my husband, whose love I possess,/ To the care of my daughters, whom Heaven will bless...'. She liked *Pride and Prejudice* better than *Mansfield Park*, she responded to Mrs Norris but found Fanny vapid, and Mr Collins and Lady Catherine take pride of place in her appraisal of her daughter's fiction.

There follows a detailed summary of the Leigh Perrot case, Tucker stressing the fact that the Austen reaction to events is not known. Tucker feels that there is no evidence of an estrangement between the families as a result, though there is a hint in one of Jane's letters that Mrs Leigh Perrot did not visit them after her acquittal. Apparently she did not get on with Jane, but Tucker points out that she did provide an annuity of £100 from 1820 onwards for Mrs Austen 'to compensate for the loss in income she had sustained on the death of her eldest son James in 1819'.

The section on the Hampshire Austens begins with Jane's brother James, the poet of the family and the major contributor to the Steventon theatricals. There is a discriminating analysis of contributions to *The Loiterer* which, according to Tucker, 'reveals source material used by Jane in her early and even in her more mature writings'. Despite, this Tucker feels that James is the least remarkable in positive terms of the brothers; his later poems are didactic with one or two exceptions, but there is a poem 'mistakenly thought to be a description of Winchester Cathedral' which from line 23 is about James' feelings for Jane. It is an epitaph on his sister:

> In her (rare union) were combined
> A fair form and a fairer mind:
> Hers, Fancy quick and clear good sense
> And wit which never gave offence;
> A Heart as warm as ever beat,
> A Temper, even, calm and sweet …

And so on, but one feels that it has associations with the *Biographical Notice*, a required and conventional family tribute with the family in mind.

Little is said, or perhaps can be said, about George, who lived until the age of 72 and was obviously feeble-minded. Tucker takes issue with the commonly held view that Edward was adopted by his cousin Thomas Knight in childhood, demonstrating convincingly that it could not have occurred before Edward was 16. He became squire of Godmersham in 1798, when Jane and Cassandra visited him there. Very generous to his mother and sisters, he later took the name of Knight: Tucker records a typical Jane quip in a letter, 'I must learn to make a better K'. Her favourite brother was Henry, an attractive man who was unfortunately made bankrupt in 1816 and whose 'quixotic impetuosity' was a byword in the family. He was a regular contributor to *The Loiterer*, and Jane dedicated one of her burlesques to him (*Lesley Castle*). He joined the war against France in 1793, entered the Oxford Militia and married Eliza de Feuillide, who had pursued him after the death of her husband in 1794. He became successively a banker and army agent in London, thus providing his sisters with a place to stay in town. He took Jane to the theatre, including one memorable visit to see Kean as Shylock in *The Merchant of Venice*. Eliza died in April 1813. Henry conducted the financial arrangements for the publication of the four novels issued during Jane Austen's lifetime, and also for the posthumous publication of *Northanger Abbey* and *Persuasion*. Henry changed from banking to the church in 1816, served as chaplain to the British Embassy in Berlin, taught in a grammar school, published some sermons and ended as a perpetual curate, dying in 1850.

We know that Cassandra destroyed most of Jane's papers, but Tucker's investigation nonetheless seeks to establish the nature of the relationship between the sisters. He refers to Cassandra's letters to Fanny Knight after Jane's death as evidence of her deep love for her sister. Their schooling together is briefly considered, and Tucker believes in the theory that Cassandra's greatest tragedy is to be found in the death of her fiancé. Their niece Anna provides much evidence of the mutual and almost self-engrossing attachment to each other that the Austen sisters had. By 1809 both of them were settled into spinsterhood, and Tucker observes that 'The eight peaceful years at Chawton, aided by Cassandra's protective assurance, provided Jane Austen with the security in which her genius came to fruition'. Francis William, the elder brother of Jane Austen's sailor brothers, always treasured his father's *Memorandum*, sent to him when he was about to join the *Perseverance*. It is a sensitive and intelligent moral tract which Jane herself would have appreciated. Two of her early pieces are dedicated to this brother. Much later in life he was to say that some of Captain Harville's traits in *Persuasion* were drawn from him, but one of his major regrets was that he missed the battle of Trafalgar. On the birth of his eldest son, Jane wrote a poem in which she expressed the wish that the child would inherit the character and personality of his father: 'In him, in all his ways, may we/Another Francis William see!' In July 1813 Jane asked Francis' permission to use the names of the ships in which he had served in her writing, a permission which he readily gave. His career was distinguished – he was finally Admiral of the Fleet – and it is obvious from his correspondence that he fully appreciated his sister's kindness and her wit, and was perceptive in his response to her writings. Charles John is the other distinguished naval brother. In about 1801 he gave his two sisters a topaz cross, 'a characteristic act of generosity on his part that undoubtedly provided Jane Austen with the genesis of the amber cross episode in *Mansfield Park* a decade later'. He spent a long period on a North

American station, returning to England in 1811, and was greatly taken with *Emma* when it was published. He lived 38 years longer than Jane, having been promoted to Rear-Admiral in 1846.

Tucker finally concentrates on Jane Austen's role as aunt to her eleven nephews and thirteen nieces. He feels that Fanny, her favourite niece, was unkind to her when she said many years later to her younger sister that Jane Austen was 'not so *refined* as she ought to have been for her talent'. This does not seem to be so much 'an indictment of her ingratitude' as a natural expression informed with personal feeling and hindsight. Tucker goes on to describe the various relationships. There is much praise for Anna Lefroy, and Tucker disputes with Brian Southam the idea that Anna's contribution to *Sir Charles Grandison or The Happy Man* was minimal. Anna's account leads one to conclude that her relationship with her aunt became warmer as she grew older. Jane celebrated her achievements in a series of quatrains, though here one detects the authoress' celebrated irony, or at least a tongue-in-cheek appraisal of her niece. Anna's own novel was, of course, submitted to Jane for criticism as she wrote it, though she destroyed the manuscript after her aunt's death. There follows some account of James Edward Austen-Leigh (known as Edward) who first established the outline of Jane Austen's life in his *Memoir*. He was also moved to write verse on occasions, one piece in loose couplets being addressed to his aunt registering his own pride in their relationship (assuredly in the light of her literary celebrity). Tucker believes that nephew and aunt 'reached a delightful level of empathy'. James Austen's daughter Caroline Mary Craven is also accorded a place of honour in Jane Austen studies, Tucker claiming for her *My Aunt Jane Austen*, written in 1867, that it is 'one of the seminal biographical works concerning her famous aunt'. She records how well Jane Austen got on with children, reading stories or inventing them, taking part in their activities and contributing her own voice to their games. She read Caroline's poems and stories, but Caroline recalls that Aunt Jane advised her to read more and write less until she was 16. Caroline shared her aunt's

love of music, and wrote an epitaph on her which the latter
would have appreciated. Tucker's book is a careful and balanced compilation, and while not directly concerned with the
novels, it summarizes, often with a fresh evaluation or insight or discovery, the family inheritance which shaped Jane
Austen, and thus, in a major sense, contributed to her emergence as the writer she became. It is a work of integrity and
dedication and one cannot ask for more.

John Halperin's *The Life of Jane Austen* (1984) has a
Foreword in which he points out that no 'full dress life' of
Jane Austen has been undertaken since Elizabeth Jenkins'
biography in 1938. He praises Joan Rees (see pp. 91-5) whose
work, he feels, is underrated, and criticizes Lord David Cecil,
for example, whose work is overrated. His method is to begin
with Jane Austen's death and then to look back with a
probing and searching emphasis. He feels that Henry
Austen's biographical notice is part of the cover-up to
preserve the essentially pious and respectable picture
handed down to posterity, asking 'Could the family's touched-
up portrait be a faithful likeness of her who laughed so
unrestrainedly at the absurdities of her neighbours?'

The early part of the book moves back through the background and the early years. There are passing solecisms, as
at the end of the Steventon section, where we are told that
'Her [Jane Austen] form fills out, her dark eyes take on the
hazel cast of her father and her favourite brother – and she
begins to write'. Halperin has a ready ear for the modern
colloquialism – 'What sort of a teenager was this?' – while
his own range of critical reading, Mudrick, Schorer,
Southam, for instance – carries him through the *Juvenilia*
with panache. He explores the autobiographical associations
of 'Catherine', and cites Southam, who says that Catherine
'is a significant departure from the usual type of heroine
found in the *Juvenilia*'. This is followed by some astute
analysis of *Lady Susan.*

The section ends curiously when Halperin says of the
Austen family 'They had experienced at first hand her wit,
her irony, her cold-blooded judgement, her irreverence, her
occasional malice'. Despite this emphasis, Halperin is defen-

sive about her letters. He quotes H.W. Garrod's verdict on them as being 'a desert of trivialities punctuated by oases of clever malice', considering this unfair. I feel that Halperin is right, but if you are writing a life, you must have a continuing awareness of the situations, physical and psychological, of your subject. As he says, 'One always looks for signs, for clues, for explanations for Jane Austen's early and lifelong ironic detachment'. Sometimes the look is, I feel, too hard, straining for the positive conclusion. He wonders whether one or the other of her parents did not value her work, but fortunately this is not pursued.

Halperin is good on place, identifying Mr Collins' parsonage as 'an accurate picture' of the one 'at Chevening [Kent] as it existed in the 1790s'. He is, however, concerned to 'reveal' the novelist in *Pride and Prejudice*. He finds 'strains of cynicism and nastiness – strains which seem to have made up a part of Jane Austen's personality'. He even considers that some of the comedy here is black, but just when we feel that he is moving towards a 'nasty' standpoint himself, he says 'but she was by no means the bitch-monster of E.M. Forster, H.W. Garrod, D.W. Harding, Harold Nicolson, and others'. His main emphasis is that she is 'sane', but he feels, after considering *Sense and Sensibility* for example, that she is showing that she is 'wary of men', reflected in the disastrous marriages that she portrays. I am wary of accepting this kind of conclusion, and I feel that Halperin's study is not so much a life as a series of linkings, some in the critical rather than the biographical area. Keeping to *Sense and Sensibility*, he says that 'The worst element of the awful ending is of course the scene between Eleanor and Willoughby'. This is, I think, a common judgement, but perhaps it ignores Jane Austen's intention and what she is revealing of her heroine.

Halperin's look at the letters of 1799 shows Jane Austen as 'alternately light-hearted and restless, perky and distressed', a fair summary of their effect. He turns to *Northanger Abbey* ('And again the ending is bungled'), and returns to Jane Austen, underlining her own assertion of how important her work is to her. The fact that we have no letters from

1801-4 means that for 'Jane Austen adversity blanketed energy and inspiration: she wrote only when she was relatively content and secure'. His own feelings about her nature are shown by his belief that her words on the death of her father are 'uncharacteristically tender'. Subjective interpretation is always there: the chapter headed 'The Light and the Dark' opens with the words 'Jane Austen was lonely and unhappy in Southampton. She was thirty-one, and unpublished'. Settling at Chawton inspired her to return to literature again: Halperin uses Anna Austen Lefroy's account of Jane at Chawton – she was 'not especially handsome. She seemed shy with strangers, though she was animated enough with intimates'. But soon Halperin is back to his own rhetorical questions – 'Why did she court obscurity so severely? Why this passion for secrecy?' In his narrative Halperin cites much criticism and quotes at length from the *Letters* (particularly in 1813). He feels that 'the advent of nieces and nephews' was almost too much for her, and then ventures boldly into critical analogy: '*Mansfield Park* is Jane Austen's *Vanity Fair*'. He points out that nearly everyone in it is selfish and that in some ways it is an unpleasant and controversial novel. The analogy is, I think, strained.

We wonder at the emphasis, at once too sweeping and insupportable, since *Mansfield Park* is characterized by ironic observation and the warm (perhaps over-warm) association with Fanny. Having observed that 'we perceive Mary as odious throughout', Halperin investigates the 'autobiographical' content of the novel, underlining 'Jane Austen's love of nature, her dislike of urban life, and her growing neuresthenia and distaste for 'society'. At one level he sees the novel as 'a carry-over of the traumatic Bigg Wither affair in the story of Fanny Price and Henry Crawford'. Halperin's imagination here is free-ranging, but he brings himself back to Jane Austen's fiction to note that 'There is, finally, another botched ending here'.

Glances at the letters keep pace with the narrative, though sometimes I feel that the interpretation and the comment which follows it are questionable. He finds Jane Austen 'patronising, condescending and disloyal' in a letter critical of her niece Anna Lefroy, adding 'Here, perhaps, is the worst moment in Jane Austen's letters'. I think that the terms are too strong for what is actually said, which is expressive of a kind of envy and a feeling of rejection, but with a recognition of right behaviour too. Halperin gives a full context here and there is perhaps justification for his moral tone, since there is evidence of some hypocrisy in Jane Austen's attitude.

Emma and *Persuasion* are treated to the now recognizable critical put-downs, with the first suffering from the fact that the author abandons the 'scenic' method from time to time and undertakes what he refers to as 'detached, third-person summary'. I would contend that this is not a retreat, but rather the employment of a structural mode consonant with her own artistic awareness – a form of narrative sophistication. Halperin also considers the grief of Mrs Musgrove in *Persuasion*. He feels here that the authorial words used of Dick are 'strikingly cruel and malicious', and questions Jane Austen's lack of feeling as well as her lack of taste in writing them. This judgement reflects the unevenness of the book, which has positive insights, a good (sometimes intriguing) narrative flow, much speculation and some self-indulgence, as here. Unexpected though the remarks about Dick Musgrove are, the sequence shows, if anything, an expansion of Jane Austen's emotional range. What she says of Dick makes us uneasy because of its truth: her perspective on Mrs Musgrove is darkly ironic, its edge of cruelty a passing indictment of an overdone self-absorption.

Tony Tanner's *Jane Austen* (1986) is essential reading, both for its individual insights and for the width of its conception. In his Introduction, called 'Jane Austen and the Novel', he indicates her awareness of what was going on around her in the world, and stresses that, despite her Tory views, she is certainly critical of her own society in many ways. His central and most important stress is seen in his assertion that 'What really matters...is the writer's moral relation to language'. This is defined in 'all of Jane Austen's works portray a movement towards true seeing and true speaking', a comment which parallels the emphases of D.D. Devlin (see pp. 82-4). The characteristics of her novels are

'wit, ironic reflectiveness and moral intelligence'. It is definitively neat, the balance perhaps imaging Jane Austen's own
controlled and discriminating verbal structures. Her fictional structures, seen in narrative sequences, generally
follow 'the convention of marriage-as-felicitous-closure'.

Tanner relates her to her society with positive insistence,
observing that there 'has been a tendency to privatize her
work and to miss the wider implications of seemingly local
events'. He says that it is quite obvious that there was *not*
the social stability at the time which is so often claimed, and
that there were feelings that the French Revolution could
certainly happen here. There is, therefore, a transcending of
the convention in the marriage at the end of the novel, which
'offers itself as an emblem of the ideal union of property and
propriety'. His focus on her language leads him to maintain
that 'The prose tends to balance out into patterns of antithesis and parallelism', with the interesting corollary that 'Emotion is thus not denied but contained by her rhetoric'. The
subtlety is seen, I think, in the sophisticated harmony between subject and the manner of expressing it or, as Tanner
puts it, 'she is constantly enacting and re-creating a requisite
decorum and propriety in her language'. This is extended
when he observes that 'The threats to Jane Austen's society
and her language – and they are many and increase throughout her work – are essentially all from within'. By the time
she writes *Persuasion* and *Sanditon* 'the discourse is radi-
cally changed as she discerned changes, derelictions, delin-
quencies and deteriorations in her particular class'. Her
characters define themselves 'by their free indirect speech'.

The analysis of 'Anger in the Abbey' includes the statement, difficult to refute, that the fathers in Jane Austen's
novels all suffer from a similar weakness of character.

Catherine's 'wrongness dubiously arrives at rightness' and
she goes through a process of discovering and learning, in
which she is moved to get rid of her fantasies and to confront
facts. It is in this section that the range of Tanner's investigation is felt: it must be allowed that sometimes that range is
disconcertingly off Jane Austen's text (though never irrelevant, rather comparative), as when he writes two pages on

Pamela and a bracketed 12-and-a-half line paragraph on Gilles Deleuze. When he returns he makes conspicuously appropriate comments on Jane Austen's own 'very pertinent comments on the female obsession with dress', although Heidegger and Nietsche call him away again. 'Secrecy and Sickness' is concerned with *Sense and Sensibility*. It is written with verve and mixed metaphors: 'By the end all the secrets have come to the surface and, with no more mysteries to cloud the emergent geometry of the book, the appropriate marriages can all be solemnised'. This summary is underpinned by the particularities he sees, like the psychosomatic nature of Marianne's illness, and 'the problems and paradoxes involved in life in society as she knew it'. He accounts for the reader's fellow feeling with Marianne through her 'conviction that language should be used to express private feelings rather than to preserve social forms'. Speech reflects balance (witness Marianne's recovery), although he feels that the feeblest section of the novel is that which deals with Marianne at the end.

The chapter on 'Knowledge and Opinion' which examines *Pride and Prejudice*, puts forward the idea that the novel is concerned with a man's alteration of behaviour and with a girl's alteration of her mind. Elizabeth is suspect early on, when she believes that what are merely impressions – first impressions – constitute the truth. Tanner picks up on 'impressions', which he records as the key word in three of David Hume's works. But Elizabeth develops, and thus frees herself from her inherent bias. Tanner is also insistent that the reader must understand the difference between appearance and reality. Tanner says that Jane Austen makes a direct attack on Lydia's actions as a result of her (misguided) first impressions, and goes on to say that the characters are divided into two kinds – those who are absorbed in their 'roles' so as to be blinkered, and those who can move outside them and always retain their sense of awareness. Like Barbara Hardy, Tanner stresses the effect of social spaces on character.

Most studies of *Mansfield Park* begin with some consideration of Fanny, and Tanner is no exception. He immediately points out that she has few of the qualities traditionally associated with a heroine, and then proceeds to define what the novel is really about. For him it is about 'rest and restlessness, stability and change, the moving and the immovable'. He believes that we can learn a lot about the various characters from their 'attitudes towards rural life'. Perhaps the distinguishing mark of his investigation is his concern with the 'violent' prose, which describes the Portsmouth household. Further, he feels that characters can be seen in relation to Mansfield Park itself: here he considers that the categories are 'the guardians, the inheritors and the interlopers'. Sir Thomas upholds 'two of the major values in the world of the book' – 'quietness' and 'repose' – and the subtlety of the presentation is seen in the fact that 'Lady Bertram is a travesty of those values'. Tanner feels that these guardians in themselves sufficiently account for the fact 'that the legitimate inheritors go wrong'. He says too that 'The improver of the estate is also the disturber of conventional life', while the private theatricals are used to probe 'acting' and 'role-playing' for the individual and society'. There is also some brilliant commentary (and comedy in Jane Austen's joke about *Henry VIII*) on Henry Crawford's facility in reading every part perfectly from the play: 'if you can play every part equally well, how can you know who you really are?' This is obviously a psychological notation on Henry's later behaviour.

I suppose that it is natural to call the chapter on *Emma* 'The Match-Maker', and it is typical, though not glib I think, to say that 'Emma is a match-maker who meets her match – and, in a sense, her 'maker'.

As evidence of Jane Austen's awareness of the social injustice of the period Tanner refers to her insight into 'the acute miseries of the governess situation'. He stresses this by citing the exchange between Jane Fairfax and Mrs Elton. He also examines the nature of the local situation, 'the potentially abrasive or claustrophobic aspects of the community in and through which Emma must move and have her being'. He feels that she is always capable of responding to 'the real thing' (whatever that may be) when she is faced with it. Class snobbery (and not just in the heroine) is found throughout the novel, while Emma's idea of a 'gentleman' is 'very unsurely grounded and open to abuse'. Indeed it is, for Robert Martin's inherent status (as distinct from his social status) gives the lie to her prejudice and the wilful indulgence of her pride.

Tanner notes how the title word *Persuasion* embraces a variety of nuances in its meaning, and how these are all applied in the novel. But he contends that the novel – and here, of course, his main concentration is on Anne – is about the opposite word 'dissuasion', though 'persuasion' is mentioned 'at least fourteen times in the book'. There is the use of specific time, 'the end of the Napoleonic Wars', which marks a departure in Jane Austen's fiction, with the structure allowing the vital passing of time since Anne was 'persuaded' to yield over Wentworth. Tanner stresses the duality present, the past unwritten affair with Wentworth, very influential, and the present novel we are reading which absorbs it. Once more the social scene is fully explored. He believes that in *Persuasion* the social 'forces' or values have been reduced so that they have little meaning or relevance. His probing here is singularly vital. He refers to Norah Crook's deductions regarding Sir Walter Elliot's recommendation of 'Gowland's Lotion', saying that this constitutes another strand of Jane Austen's ironic sophistication. The implication is that Mrs Clay had syphilis, and in finally becoming Mr Elliot's mistress in London provides a suitable partner for that corrupt man who is also heir to Kellynch Hall. Tanner concludes a superb chapter by altering Jane Austen's finely balanced irony at the expense of Lady Russell to 'There was nothing less for English society to do, than to admit that it had been completely wrong...'. We are a long way from the authors of the *Biographical Notice*, the *Memoir* and the 1913 biography – one wonders what they would have made of this or of the mention of a lotion which was used for its curative treatment of venereal disease.

Disease is revealed again in the analysis of *Sanditon*. Here it is the 'disease of activity'. Tanner again examines the title 'sandy-town', with its shifting emphasis which is itself a

negation. Tanner is inevitably expansive, recording Jane
Austen's exposure of advertising, profit, business (with another play on the word); he also finds that Charlotte Heywood
is a departure from her usual type of heroine. A telling
consideration reveals 'the discourses of literary appreciation
or criticism'. Sir Edward Denham 'speaks wholly in quotations...but mutilated and confused quotations which dis-
figure and maim the original texts'. The advance, or at least
the breaking of new ground which others have drawn attention to, is here given disciplined definition: 'The style is
perfectly appropriate and adapted to the new world she is
describing'. He points out that there is no reversion to earlier
modes (though his tone here seems to me to be somewhat
extreme): 'She lets the endless talkers talk endlessly, without
the interposition of her monitoring, adjudicating voice'. The
implication is progression, or at least difference successfully
achieved. He even sees the 'abrupt termination' as 'appropriate'. His conclusion is insistently unequivocal: 'Never
properly 'built', it is always a building. It is potentially simply
everywhere, and arguably is ever more rapidly becoming so.
Starting, effectively, with an overturned carriage, it presages
and foreshadows an overturned world. For one cannot diag-
nose 'a disease of activity' without suggesting the activity of
disease.' The emphasis, give or take the non-literary evaluation, is correct. Tanner's book is an original study, shedding
new light, suggesting interpretations, further evidence in
itself of the sustained complexity of Jane Austen's art and
concerns.

Park Honan's *Jane Austen: Her Life* (1987) is written on
an ambitious scale, though its claim that no-one has tried to
assimilate the new material would be contested by John
Halperin, whose biography came out in 1984 (see pp. 111-14).
He asserts that those closest to Jane Austen were responsible
for 'feeding her imagination, expanding her awareness'. It is
for this reason that so much of his study concentrates on the
family foreground of her life. Thus the Prelude – 'Frank
Austen's ride' – seeks to establish the period realism, although it is somewhat undermined by period romance. Of
Jane Austen's early life, for example, the period at the Abbey

School in Reading, Honan sometimes fashions the fictional thrust as well as the scholarly fact: 'At nine and ten she was a timid, imitative observer hovering near a circle of slangy, half-sophisticated girls who talked over her head and laughed at everything'. Fortunately this kind of indulgence disappears. There is a valuable discussion of the influence of *Sir Charles Grandison* on the youthful Jane Austen, as well as a revaluation of the character of Mrs Lefroy, 'misinterpreted by biographers who have not read her diary and letters'.

There is an astute focus on James and Henry Austen's Oxford publication *The Loiterer* and its connections with Jane Austen and her later writings. Honan says that she sent James a humorous letter (with the signature 'Sophia Sentiment') which he printed. She found their work useful and stimulating because of its adoption of Richardsonian morality (in *Sir Charles Grandison*). Honan also draws attention to the fact that her brothers' journal covered so much in which she delighted, such as jokes, elegance, the specifics of language, and the limitations of popular fiction.

The influence of her father and his concern for his children is indicated (he enlisted Warren Hastings' influence for Frank), there is some analysis of the *Juvenilia*, while Jane's interest in dancing is stressed. She and her sister watched the matrimonial affairs (and their economic dependence) with amusement; Jane's fondness for ironic observation as a young woman surfaced into the later writings. Her brother James' financial plight ('a clergyman of slender means') provided material for *Sense and Sensibility* and *Pride and Prejudice*, but Honan registers the effects of the French Revolution on the family through Eliza de Feuillide's experiences and, more peacefully, evidence of Jane Austen's interest in music, observing 'Love songs relieved and delighted her, even soppy ones'. He goes on to say that 'She believed in love, and used merciless realism against a world that threatened it, though she knew that love is comic itself'.

Eliza's 'exploits' provided her with the basis, the long story in letters, which 'her nephew later called *Lady Susan*'. Honan's own critical insight and sophistication are evident here: 'This novel seems more subversively anti-social than critics understand', the fact that she didn't try to print it suggesting to him 'that she knew how attractive she had made her masterly villainess'. In her own life Honan speaks of the affected literary man, Sir Egerton Brydges, and weighs up her relationship with Tom Lefroy, about which there has been so much speculation. He says, 'She had decided to fall in love, and she saw little at any time to make her regret that decision', though she later mocks herself (or perhaps affects to mock herself) by saying 'I do not care sixpence' for him. In her early twenties there is the affair with Samuel Blackall, who 'lunged in serious pursuit' of her. There is a very interesting deduction about *First Impressions* (the early draft of *Pride and Prejudice*) and its relationship to the outside world of mutiny and war: 'This moral and comic story was her *war* – with no heroism – and the version she wrote between October 1796 and August 1797 probably used Elizabeth Bennet as chief narrator and interpreter'. This would account for her close identification with Elizabeth.

One of the most refreshing aspects of Honan's work is his ability to reinterpret with enlightenment. He says of Jane Austen's celebrated remark about the woman delivered of a still-born baby 'That was tasteless and cruel, exuberant and healthy. It defied life and laughed at death'. This is an over-statement, but it needfully redresses the malicious balance of some critics. Honan stresses that she was always adept at the informal joke, sometimes sick, and that she was aware of the undercurrents of society politenesses 'that gave women fixed roles'. Honan traces factual sources, for example, with *Northanger Abbey*, where Eliza de Feuillide's experience in a doctor's surgery gave Jane Austen the idea for the 'Gothic horrors' of Catherine's discovery in the novel. And as always there are some superb critical pointings, such as 'What is weak in *Northanger Abbey* is its freshest and most innovative feature – its narrative voice. That voice was the last feature of her art that Jane Austen developed'. Other interesting identifications include her brother Frank's reportage of the lashing of men on his ship for the 'unnatural crime of sodomy', which is referred to in Mary Crawford's remark 'of *Rears*, and Vices, I saw enough'. Though dubious, this *is* possible, conferring perhaps a coarser dimension on Jane Austen (and on Mary Crawford). Frank was unmoved by Nelson's adultery, which occasioned national debate, and Honan maintains that 'Frank's sister herself was intrigued by sexual infidelity'.

Most biographers agree that the move from Steventon in May 1801 was traumatic. But the main events in her life thereafter would seem to be Harris Wither's proposal (2 December 1802), with her initial acceptance and retraction on the following day, and her visit to Lyme which was to provide so much substance for *Persuasion*. Mrs Lefroy died on 16th December 1804, Jane Austen's 29th birthday, and four years later she wrote a moving poem about her. The emphasis on her immediate circle as she enters her thirties is interesting. Honan believes that 'No one in her family had a high idea of her novel-writing', despite the 'sensible and flexible language' she employed and the 'psychological depths' she was plumbing. He feels that she may have witnessed the tension between James and his second wife and used it for the exchanges between Mr and Mrs Bennett when she came to revise *First Impressions*; James' attacks on novels ensured that her own fictional efforts were kept in perspective. He yearned for the Oxford life which was denied him, but he had a good relationship with Jane, though she was irritated by him at times, and Frank was so outwardly decent that she was also irritated by him. Honan subtly analyses the relationship between Jane and these brothers, rejecting the previous simplistic appraisals. Jane's delight in Martha Lloyd is also revealed, and her verses to her brother Frank on the birth of a boy to his wife Mary are quoted: 'Thy infant days may he inherit,/ Thy warmth, nay insolence of spirit.' The spirit in her own writing here is obvious, and Honan observes that in her room at Chawton 'she produced the most delightful comedy in our language since Shakespeare'. Honan's perspective throughout is admirable: his picture is of a complex but integrated person, not a paragon. As he says, 'There is no greater contrast in Jane Austen's writings than that between her sharp, comically malicious letters and the

Christian prayers she composed'. He adds that to reconcile 'her faith with her fury' she resorted to her 'fictional comedies', working out her energies without personal attack, though 'life itself is recreated and appraised for every reader'.

The geographical centrality of Chawton is stressed, and Honan finds 'a new social conscience evident' in the novels she revised and wrote there. As for her personality at this time, Honan quotes from a letter (by Charlotte-Maria Middleton) which only came to light in 1985 – 'She was a most kind and enjoyable person to *children* but somewhat stiff and cold to strangers'. Honan places great emphasis on her 'stoical Christian faith', saying that 'This is what gives her comedies "their moral confidence" '. There is some fine research investigation of other senses and sensibilities – 'one might think that many authors were writing Jane Austen's novel before she did' – and a forthright appraisal of Marianne. I have said earlier that Honan the biographer produces stimulating critical judgements, and here he observes of *Sense and Sensibility* that 'Music, the tones of human talk, noise and silence are so prominent that the novel is nearly a discourse on sound'. But it is, nonetheless, the darkest of her comedies.

The years 1811-13 are given a full personal treatment as to the publication of *Pride and Prejudice*, but the social background absorbs Honan, and the suffering and the sick of the period are researched too. Nevertheless '*Pride and Prejudice* is a smart celebration of the reign'. There is a fascinating aside on Jane's 'larking about' in the Steventon marriage register, which recorded 'The Banns of Marriage between Henry Frederick Howard Fitzwilliam of London and Jane Austen of Steventon'. We are going back in time of course, but Honan feels that this shows that 'even at twenty' she had 'portrayed some perceived aspects of herself in Elizabeth'. Looking at *Pride and Prejudice* he picks out the tone of the novel as being 'Elizabeth's', and notes the echo of Mercutio in Bingley's 'Come, Darcy, I must have you dance'. He refers to the 'hegemony of men' in the novel, suggests that its 'three solemn reviews do not tell the *whole* story of its reception', and that 'Its deepest subject is happiness'.

Honan covers 1813-14 in the same depth. Thus Charles'
wife Fanny who raised 'three children aboard ship' provides
the original for Mrs Croft in *Persuasion*, while the tone of the
times – the connection with the Regent – leads him to believe
that 'adultery in high places is generally reflected in the
Crawford—Rushworth affair in her work'. He sorts out the
remark on 'Ordination' and the misinterpretations of Jane
Austen's emphasis here very well indeed. Always there are
interesting identifications, as with 'Fanny Price is the name
of Crabbe's own "weakly firm" heroine in *The Parish Register*'. Jane Austen shows a special interest in 'passivity', reflected in Lady Bertram in *Mansfield Park*, while Fanny at
Sotherton 'expresses the author's own early immature Tory
romanticism'. The *Lover's Vows* rehearsals expose the morals
of the participants – 'they do *not* act but express real feelings'.
He points out that Jane refused to let Cassandra influence
her into having Henry marry Fanny, and he praises the
realism of their relationship. He feels, though, that Fanny is
'gently mocked' by her author, and notes, as many others
have, the strange fact that there were not reviews (or any
that we know of) of *Mansfield Park*.

After her niece Anna's marriage to Ben Lefroy Jane finds
herself acting as consultant, and from this we learn her
celebrated views on fiction and the self-imposed limitations
of her own practice. *Emma* is treated in some detail, from its
family in-joke to the fondness for word-play which they all
shared and which informs the novel. The overall analysis of
Emma is perceptive, even definitive, with Highbury central
to 'intense themes', where Jane Fairfax's position could lead
to 'slavery' in the 'governess trade', and where Mr Elton's
complacency is reflective of the church failing its lower ord-
ers. Perhaps the novel's most significant scene, the visit to
Box Hill, is 'secular, savage, split and uneasy'.

Invited to Carlton House by James Clarke, she found
herself fêted when she was nearly forty, but at the same time
she attended meticulously to her work, sending John Murray
a marked copy for the second edition of *Mansfield Park* with
'new naval details for her Portsmouth scenes', while she
made other minor changes. When he turns to *Persuasion*,

Honan notes that it is 'an emotionally complex novel' and that she 'brings tragic feelings to bear on comedy'. He feels that to Anne Mrs Smith 'is a dark mirror-image of herself', and records the essentially balanced treatment of Lady Russell, from reprimand to respect for her 'good and loving intentions'.

The final phase of Jane Austen's life is covered with sympathy, insight and sensitivity. Honan feels that as she became more ill 'she used her wit as a defence against pity she did not want'. Her success is perhaps measured by the fact that '*Sanditon* is very remarkably vigorous' and by the trenchant artistry of her humour, shown in 'I have read *The Corsair*, mended my petticoat, and have nothing else to do'. Honan's complete identification with his subject runs beyond the narrative text: Appendix B summarizes acutely 'A Selection of Studies relating to Jane Austen'. It sets the seal on a dedicated investigation.

Claudia Johnson's *Jane Austen: Women, Politics and the Novel* (1988) takes issue with much previous criticism and interpretation of Jane Austen. Although Margaret Anne Doody considers it 'brilliant, witty and well-informed', it seems heavy in the utterance and sometimes doubtful in its conclusions. Here is a definitive assertion from the Introduction: 'The precondition of Austen's posthumous admittance into the canon was the apparent contentment to work artfully within carefully constricted boundaries which have been termed "feminine" '. Miss Johnson reviews Jane Austen criticism and scholarship, putting down Chapman, whom she considers more antiquarian than scholarly, and telling us that the generality of appraisals 'has implied that her novels are off limits to the ponderous diction of literary scholarship'. The phrasing here seems to me to be somewhat 'off limits' in its emphasis. Despite other generalizations, however, Miss Johnson evaluates positively and relatively, saying that Jane Austen's fiction 'emerges, draws and departs from a largely feminine tradition of political novels, novels which are highly informed and often distinctively flexible, rather than ferociously partisan in their sympathies'. In this study Miss Johnson's style sometimes inhibits our direct understanding of the quality of what she is saying. After summarizing the situation in which 'The Revolution in France gave rise to the novel of crisis in England', she contends that 'Austen may slacken the desperate tempos employed by her more strenuously politicised counterparts, but she shares their artistic strategies and their commitment to uncovering the ideological underpinnings of cultural myths'. A pity that it cannot be more simply put, though when she gets to Jane Austen's own works and their affiliations, she writes with verve and directness on occasions. When Jane Austen began *Northanger Abbey* some time in the mid-1790s, 'the gothic novel had already been thoroughly imbued with political implications, and here in turning her powers of parody to a saliently politicised form, Austen raised the stakes on her work'. This stylistic solecism almost diminishes the point. Miss Johnson feels that Henry Tilney 'simply believes that he knows women's minds better than they do', ignoring the obvious corollary that Jane Austen knows Henry Tilney's mind and reveals it without judgemental bias. There is some good writing on *Northanger Abbey*, though, and I feel that Miss Johnson is right when she says that 'Gothic novels teach the deferent and self-deprecating Catherine to do what no one and nothing else does: to distrust paternal figures and to feel that her power of refusal is continuously under siege' and 'Breaking engagements and words of honour of all sorts is the predominant activity of *Northanger Abbey*'. There are some shrewd comments on *Sense and Sensibility*, which contains much 'progressive social criticism' and also 'tends to be the locus of venal and idle habits' as regards the family. Miss Johnson urges us not to underestimate Elizabeth's role and attitudes in *Pride and Prejudice*, telling us that in this novel 'passing happiness is the business of life'. But all too often the emphasis is odd, as in 'Unless we acknowledge that Darcy's pride is a "criminal" assault on Elizabeth's happiness, we will not appreciate the profundity of his eventual transformation'. Elizabeth is seen as radical, asserting that 'the interests of the ruling class' cannot be 'morally binding upon her'. She challenges 'the power of rank and wealth', and through her Jane Austen was attempting 'to reform gentry myths'. This is the conclusion to the chapter on *Pride and Prejudice*: in this novel 'alone Austen consents to conservative myths, but only in order to possess them and to ameliorate them from within, so that the institutions that they vindicate can bring about, rather than inhibit, the expansion and fulfillment of happiness'.

Miss Johnson is directly bold on *Mansfield Park*, where Sir Thomas is seen as 'the most assiduous of actors', and where the author 'parodies the structures of conservative fiction most subversively, though in some ways most obliquely of all, in its presentation of family itself'. Here the detailed appraisal suggests that Sir Thomas' '*paternal* affection' for Fanny is not exempt 'from an aura of erotic implication'. This may give us pause, but it is not without foundation. Stylistic warts continue to appear on the critical flesh, as in 'Emma assumes her own entitlement to independence and power...and in doing so she poaches on what is felt to be male turf'. The novel is 'a cagey celebration' of female writing, and among other things 'suggests that Emma has not misread Harriet after all, and that, on the contrary, other people have'. These provocative, independent judgements continue on *Persuasion*, where 'the landed classes have not lost their power, they have lost their prestige and their moral authority for the heroine'. Miss Johnson also talks of 'Anne's indifference to filial property' over her visit to Mrs Smith, and asserts that 'stately houses and their proprietors are no longer formidable, and their intransigence is matched only by their vapidity'. Jane Austen questioned 'conservative fiction' in such a way that 'its most cherished mythologies' would never be recovered. Miss Johnson's arguments are sometimes, one feels, a little strained, but there is some inspirational interpretation in her work. Unfortunately, Roger Gard's sane, humane, intelligent and perceptive *Jane Austen's Novels: The Art of Clarity* (Yale and London, 1992) was published too late for me to include detail here, but of its importance and quality I have no doubt.

Conclusion

As I indicated at the outset, any selection of material, whether critical, biographical or scholarly (or all three), is largely arbitrary and inevitably subjective. If the early appraisals are relatively straightforward in their approach and in their conclusions, it is certainly true that the beginnings of disciplined and imaginative evaluation of Jane Austen are given a marked impetus from the mid-20th century onwards. There has been an increasing sophistication and subtlety of examination. My own view is that, with one or two exceptions well before her own time – one thinks of Simpson and Farrer – the major contribution to the fuller interpretation of Jane Austen's work is that of Mary Lascelles. She has been followed by other expansive interpretations which reflect a deepening historical awareness and perspective, but it must be said that Jane Austen lends herself to critics who wish to score polemical points or to see her as evincing some kind of convenient typicality.

I make no apology for including so much biographical material – particularly on the family who were so important in making her the writer she became. Tucker and Park Honan have made invaluable contributions to the understanding of her life; in Honan's case, his scholarly dedication and inspirational critical insights and links ensure, I feel, that his biography will not be superseded. R.W. Chapman and Miss Lascelles have a worthy successor, too, in Brian Southam. His investigations, from manuscripts to critical anthologies and his own interpretations, have defined and stabilized Jane Austen's now unassailable status. Much feminist criticism has provided new perspectives, a questioning of attitudes, and some fine and provocatively sympathetic critical insights. The directions of appraisal in the future, however, while they may look back to our present judgements and the judgements of the past with respect or disdain, will inevitably be different. Emphases, like fashions in criticism, are subject to the influences which herald change.

In 1987 J.F. Burrows published an intriguing book called *Computation into Criticism: A Study of Jane Austen's Novels and an Experiment in Method*. Burrows states that characters in her novels differ in their use of words such as 'the', 'of', 'it' and 'I', and further that 'In some cases the frequencies change as the characters develop'.

The methods of statistical analysis are here applied to literature, and this leads to an unequivocal assertion: '*From no other evidence* than a statistical analysis of the relative frequencies of the very common words, it is possible to differentiate sharply and appropriately among the ideolects of Jane Austen's characters and even to trace the ways in which an ideolect can develop in the course of a novel.' I have chosen, perhaps through prejudice or irreverent pride, not to try to evaluate Burrows' work, but I have to acknowledge that it is a substantial piece of research, and I have little doubt that it could be extended both within the compass of Jane Austen's language and of course widely to other writers. Those who write criticism, or who merely try to summarize it, as here, always have to be prepared to learn a new terminology, from the simple descriptive, analytic or practical, through the New Criticism, Feminism, Structuralism and Deconstruction to 'An Experiment in Method'. The one constant throughout the changes is the writer under examination. Jane Austen's novels have survived, indeed triumphed, over phases of critical and popular taste. It may be safely asserted that they manufacture criticism without in any way undermining the strength and permanence of their critical hold. I go back to Barbara Hardy's opening remark and refashion it slightly: great artists transcend their chosen genre by the qualities of their literary personality and practice.

Bibliography

This is divided as follows:

A. Works by Jane Austen
B. Biographical, Critical and Scholarly books or articles on Jane Austen.

A. Works by Jane Austen

Major Works: (First publication)

Sense and Sensibility, 3 vols (Thomas Egerton, Whitehall, October 1811)
Pride and Prejudice, 3 vols (Thomas Egerton, Whitehall, January 1813;
 2nd edn, October 1813; 3rd edn, 1817)
Mansfield Park, 3 vols (Thomas Egerton, Whitehall, May 1814; 2nd edn,
 John Murray, February 1816)
Emma, 3 vols (John Murray, December 23rd 1815; dated 1816)
Northanger Abbey and *Persuasion*, 4 vols (John Murray, December 1817;
 dated 1818)

Minor Works:

Volume the First (ed. R.W. Chapman, Oxford, 1933); *Volume the Second*
 (London, 1922); *Volume the Third* (Oxford, 1954)

Annotated Editions:

*The Novels of Jane Austen: The Text Based on Collation of the Early
 Editions*, 5 vols (ed. R.W. Chapman, Oxford, 1923). Frequently reprinted and revised (by Mary Lascelles and others). The *Minor Works*
 (see above) were included complete in an additional volume, the set
 having become *The Oxford Illustrated Jane Austen*.
World's Classics, 6 vols (Oxford University Press, 1971), re-issued with
 new introductions in 1990 (contains explanatory notes).

Penguin English Library (now *Penguin Classics*), 6 vols (Penguin, 1965-
80). Critical introductions and explanatory notes.
Both the above editions have introductions by distinguished Jane Austen
scholars and are strongly recommended.
Also recommended is the Virago edition, 5 vols (1989), with introductions by Margaret Drabble.

Note: The *Letters*, and, for example, B.C. Southam's edition of Jane
Austen's *Sir Charles Grandison* are included in section B. below. For fuller
treatment of contemporary and modern criticism readers are referred to
the two volumes in the admirable Critical Heritage and Casebook series,
all of which are listed in the following section.

B. Critical Bibliography

Amis, Kingsley, 'What Became of Jane Austen?', *Spectator* (4 October,
1957) pp. 33-40
Andrews, P.B.S, 'The Date of *Pride and Prejudice*', *Notes and Queries* 213
(1968) pp. 338-42
Auerbach, Nina, 'Jane Austen and Romantic Imprisonments', in David
Monaghan (ed.), *Jane Austen in a Social Context* (London, 1981)
Austen, Henry, 'Biographical Notice' in *Northanger Abbey* and *Persuasion*
(London, 1818; revised 1832)
Austen-Leigh, Emma, *Jane Austen and Steventon* (London, 1937)
Austen-Leigh, J.E, *A Memoir of Jane Austen* (London, 1871)
Austen-Leigh, Mary Augusta, *Personal Aspects of Jane Austen* (London,
1920)
Austen-Leigh, William, and Richard Arthur, *Jane Austen: Her Life and
Letters, a Family Record* (London, 1913)
Babb, Howard, *Jane Austen's Novels: The Fabric of Dialogue* (Columbus,
Ohio, 1962)
Bayley, John, 'Charactisation in Jane Austen', in J. David Grey (ed.), *The
Jane Austen Handbook* (1986) pp. 24-34
Bennett, Arnold, *Evening Standard* (July, 1927)
Brabourne, Lord Edward, *Letters of Jane Austen*, 2 vols (London, 1884)
Bradbury, Malcolm, 'Jane Austen's *Emma*', in David Lodge (ed.), *'Emma':
A Casebook* (London, 1968)
Bradbrook, Frank, *Jane Austen and her Predecessors* (Cambridge, 1966)
Booth, Wayne, 'Control of Distance in Jane Austen's *Emma*', in David
Lodge (ed.), *'Emma': A casebook* (London, 1968)
Bowen, Elizabeth, *'Persuasion'*, *London Magazine* IV (June 1957) pp. 47-51

Bower, Reuben, *The Fields of Light* (London, 1961)

Bradley, A.C., 'Jane Austen: A Lecture', in *Essays and Studies by Members of the English Association* 2 (1911) pp. 7-36

Brontë, Charlotte, 'Nothing Profound', in David Lodge (ed.), *'Emma': A Casebook* (London, 1968)

Brophy, Bridget, Introduction to *Pride and Prejudice* (London, 1967)

Brown, Julia Prewitt, *Jane Austen's Novels: Social Change and Literary Form* (Cambridge, 1979)

Brown, Lloyd W., 'Jane Austen: The Feminist Tradition', *Nineteenth-Century Fiction* 28 (1973-4) pp. 321-38

Bush, Douglas, *Jane Austen* (London, 1975)

Butler, Marilyn, *Jane Austen and the War of Ideas* (Oxford, 1975; revised 1987)

Butler, Marilyn, *Romantics, Rebels and Reactionaries: English Literature and Its Background 1760-1830* (Oxford, 1981)

Carpenter, Thomas Edward, *The Story of Jane Austen's Home* (Chawton, 1954; re-issued 1983)

Cecil, Lord David, *A Portrait of Jane Austen* (Penguin, 1978)

Chapman, R.W. (ed.), *The Novels of Jane Austen*, 5 vols (Oxford, 1923)

——— *Jane Austen's Letters* (Oxford 1932; re-issued 1952)

——— *Jane Austen: Facts and Problems* (Oxford, 1948)

——— *Jane Austen: A Critical Bibliography* (Oxford, 1953)

Chesterton, G.K., *The Victorian Age in Literature* (London, 1913)

Collected Reports of the Jane Austen Society, 3 vols (1949-65, 1966-75, 1976-85, Yield House, Hants)

Craik, Wendy, *Jane Austen: The Six Novels* (London, 1965)

——— *Jane Austen in her Time* (London, 1969)

Crane, R.S., *The Idea of the Humanities and Other Essays, Critical and Historical* (Notre Dame, 1967) pp. 283-302

Devlin, D.D., *Jane Austen and Education* (London, 1975)

Donoghue, Denis, 'A View of *Mansfield Park*', in B.C. Southam (ed.), *Critical Essays on Jane Austen* (London, 1968) pp. 39-59

Duckworth, Alistair M., *The Improvement of the Estate* (London, 1971)

Farrer, Reginald, 'Jane Austen, July 18, 1817', *Quarterly Review* 228 (1917) pp. 1-30

Fergus, Jan, *Jane Austen and the Didactic Novel* (London, 1983)

Fleishman, Avrom, *A Reading of 'Mansfield Park': An Essay in Critical Synthesis* (Minneapolis, 1967)

——— '*Mansfield Park* in Its Time', *Nineteenth-Century Fiction* 22 (1967-8) pp. 1-18

Forster, E.M., Review of the Chapman editions, *Nation and Athenaeum* 34 (1923-4) pp. 512-14; reprinted in *Abinger Harvest* (1936)

_____ 'Sanditon', *The Nation* (March 21, 1925); reprinted in *Abinger Harvest* (1936) pp. 152-55

Freeman, Jean, *Jane Austen in Bath* (Alton, 1969)

Gard, Roger, *Jane Austen's Novels: The Art of Clarity* (New Haven and London, 1992)

Gilbert, Sandra, and Gubar, Susan, *The Madwoman in the Attic* (New Haven and London, 1981)

Gilson, David, *A Bibliography of Jane Austen* (Oxford, 1982)

Gray, J. David (ed.), *The Jane Austen Handbook* (Athlone Press, 1982)

Greene, D.J., 'Jane Austen and the Peerage', *PMLA* 68 (1953) pp. 1017-31

Halperin, John (ed.), *Jane Austen: Bicentenary Essays* (Cambridge and New York, 1975)

_____ *Jane Austen: Her Life* (Macmillan, 1984)

Harding, D.W., 'Regulated Hatred: An Aspect of the Work of Jane Austen', *Scrutiny* 8 (1939-40) pp. 346-62

_____ 'Character and Caricature in Jane Austen', in B.C. Southam (ed.), *Critical Essays on Jane Austen* (London, 1968) pp. 83-105

Hardy, Barbara, *A Reading of Jane Austen* (London, 1975)

Harvey, W.J., 'The Plot of *Emma*', in David Lodge (ed.), *'Emma': A Casebook* (London, 1968)

Hayes, E.N., '*Emma*: A Dissenting Opinion', in David Lodge (ed.), *'Emma': A Casebook* (London, 1968)

Hill, Constance, *Jane Austen, Her Homes and Friends* (London, 1902)

Hodge, Jane Aiken, *The Double Life of Jane Austen* (London, 1972)

Honan, Park, *Jane Austen: Her Life* (London, 1987)

Hopkins, Annette B., 'Jane Austen the Critic', *PMLA* 40 (1925) pp. 398-425

Hough, Graham, 'Narrative and Dialogue in Jane Austen', *Critical Quarterly* 12 (1970) pp. 201-29

Howells, William Dean, *Criticism and Fiction* (London and New York, 1891)

_____ *Heroines of Fiction* (London and New York, 1901)

_____ 'On the Immortality of Jane Austen', *Harper's Magazine* 127 (1913) pp. 958-61

Hubback, John H., and Edith C., *Jane Austen's Sailor Brothers* (London and New York, 1906)

Hughes, R.E., 'The Education of Emma Woodhouse', in David Lodge (ed.), *'Emma': A Casebook* (London, 1968)

Hutton, R.H., 'The Charm of Miss Austen', *Spectator* 64 (1890) pp. 403-4

James, Henry, 'The Lesson of Balzac', in Leon Edel (ed.), *The House of Fiction* (London, 1957) pp. 60-85

Jenkins, Elizabeth, *Jane Austen: A Biography* (London, 1938)

Johnson, Claudia L., *Women, Politics and the Novel* (Chicago, 1988)

Kavanagh, Julia, *English Women of Letters* (London, 1862)

Kettle, Arnold, *'Emma'*, in David Lodge (ed.), *'Emma': A Casebook* (London, 1968)

Kirkham, Margaret, *Jane Austen, Feminism and Fiction* (Brighton, 1983)

Lascelles, Mary, *Jane Austen and Her Art* (London and Oxford, 1939)

Laski, Marghanita, *Jane Austen and Her World* (London, 1969)

Leavis, F.R., *The Great Tradition* (London, 1948)

Leavis, Q.D., 'A Critical Theory of Jane Austen's Writings', *Scrutiny* 10 (1941-42) pp. 61-75

Le Faye, Deidre, *Jane Austen: A Family Record* (London, 1989)

Lerner, Laurence, *The Truthtellers: Jane Austen, George Eliot, D.H. Lawrence* (London and New York, 1967)

Lewes, G.H., 'Recent Novels: French and English', *Fraser's Magazine* 36 (1847) pp. 686-95

Lewis, C.S., 'A Note on Jane Austen', *Essays in Criticism* 4 (1954) pp. 359-71

Liddell, Robert, *The Novels of Jane Austen* (London, 1963)

Litz, A. Walton, 'The Chronology of *Mansfield Park*', *Notes and Queries*, 208 (1961) pp. 221-2

―――― *Jane Austen: A Study of her Artistic Development* (London, 1965)

Lodge, David (ed.), *'Emma': A Casebook* (London, 1968)

―――― *The Language of Fiction* (London and New York, 1966)

Macaulay, T.B. Baron, Letter to Hannah M. Macaulay, August 1831, in G.O. Trevelyan, *The Life and Letters of Lord Macaulay*, vol. 1 (London, 1876) p. 240

―――― Letter 18 July 1831, in Thomas Pinney (ed.), *The Letters of Macaulay*, vol II (London, 1974) p. 72

McMaster, Juliet (ed.), *The Achievement of Jane Austen* (London, 1976)

―――― *Jane Austen on Love* (London, 1978)

Malden, S.F., *Jane Austen* (London, 1889)

Moers, Ellen, *Literary Women* (London, 1978)

Moler, Kenneth L., *Jane Austen's Art of Allusion* (Lincoln, USA, 1968)

Monaghan, David, *Jane Austen and Social Vision* (London, 1980)

Morgan, Susan, *In the Meantime: Character and Perception in Jane Austen's Fiction* (Chicago, 1980)

Mudrick, Marvin, *Jane Austen: Irony as Defense and Discovery* (Princeton and London, 1952)

Nardin, Jane, 'Children and their Families in Jane Austen's Novels', in Janet Todd (ed.), *Jane Austen: New Perspectives*, Woman and Literature. N.S. 3 (New York and London, 1983) pp. 73-87

Oliphant, Margaret, Article in *Blackwood's Edinburgh Magazine* (March 1870)

Page, Norman, *The Language of Jane Austen*, (London, 1972)

Paris, Bernard J., *Character and Conflict in Jane Austen's Novels: A Psychological Approach* (Detroit, 1977)

Pellew, George, *Jane Austen's Novels* (Boston, 1883)

Pevsner, Nikolaus, 'The Architectural Setting of Jane Austen's Novels', *Journal of the Warburg and Courtauld Institutes* 31 (1968) pp. 404-22

Phillipps, Kenneth, *The Language of Jane Austen* (London, 1970)

Pinion, F.B., *A Jane Austen Companion* (London, 1973)

Pollock, W.F., 'British Novelists – Richardson, Miss Austen, Scott', *Frasers Magazine* (January 1860) pp. 30-35

Repplier, Agnes, 'Literary Shibboleths', *Atlantic Monthly* (May 1890)

———— 'Conversation in Novels', in her *Essays in Miniature* (New York, 1892)

———— 'Jane Austen', *Critic* 37 (1900) pp. 514-5

Raleigh, Sir Walter, *The English Novel* (London and New York, 1894)

Rees, Joan, *Jane Austen, Woman and Writer* (London, 1976)

Roberts, Warren, *Jane Austen and the French Revolution* (London, 1979)

Saintsbury, George, Preface to *Pride and Prejudice* (London, 1894); reprinted in his *Prefaces and Essays* (London 1933) pp. 194-209

Sampson, George, Review of the Chapman editions, *Bookman* 65 (1924) pp. 191-3

Schorer, Mark, 'The Humiliation of Emma Woodhouse', *Literary Review* 2 (1959); reprinted in Ian Watt (ed.), *Jane Austen: A Collection of Critical Essays* (New Jersey, 1963)

Scott, Sir Walter, Unsigned article in *Quarterley Review* XIV (October 1815)

———— 'Journal' (14th March 1826), in J.G. Tait (ed.), *Journal of Walter Scott, 1825-6* (1939) p. 135

Shannon, Edgar F., '*Emma*: Character and Construction', in David Lodge (ed.), '*Emma': A Casebook* (London,1968)

Simpson, Richard, Review of *Memoir*, in B.C. Southam(ed.), *Jane Austen: The Critical Heritage* I (London, 1968) pp. 241-65

Smith, Goldwin, *Life of Jane Austen* (London, 1890)

Smithers, D.W., *Jane Austen in Kent* (Westerham, 1982)

Southam, B.C. (ed.), *Jane Austen's 'Sir Charles Grandison'* (Oxford, 1980)

———— *Jane Austen's Literary Manuscripts* (Oxford, 1964)

———— (ed.), *Critical Essays on Jane Austen* (London, 1968)

———— (ed.), *Jane Austen: The Critical Heritage*, vol. I (1968); vol. II (1985)

Stephen, Sir Leslie, 'Jane Austen', *DNB* II (London, 1885) pp. 259-60

Tanner, Tony, *Jane Austen* (London, 1986)

Thackeray, Anne, 'Jane Austen', *Cornhill Magazine* (1871) pp. 158-74

Tave, Stuart M., *Some Words of Jane Austen* (Chicago and London, 1973)

Todd, Janet (ed.), *Jane Austen: New Perspectives*, Women and Literature N.S. 3 (New York, 1983)

Trilling, Lionel, 'In Mansfield Park', in his *The Opposing Self* (London and New York, 1955) pp. 206-30

——— 'Emma and the Legend of Jane Austen', in his *Beyond Culture* (London and New York, 1965) pp. 31-55

Trollope, A., 'Miss Austen's Timidities', in David Lodge (ed.), *'Emma': A Casebook* (London, 1968)

Tucker, George Holbert, *A Goodly Heritage: A History of Jane Austen's Family* (Manchester, 1983)

Van Ghent, Dorothy, 'On *Pride and Prejudice*', in *The English Novel: Form and Function* (New York, 1953)

Ward, Mrs Humphrey, Review of Lord Brabourne's edition of the Letters, *Macmillan's Magazine* 51 (1884) pp. 84-91

Watt, Ian, 'Sense triumphantly introduced to Sensibility', Introduction to the novel (1961), reproduced in B.C. Southam (ed.), *'Sense and Sensibility', 'Pride and Prejudice' and 'Northanger Abbey': A Casebook* (1976)

——— *The Rise of the Novel* (London, 1957)

——— (ed.), *Jane Austen: A Collection of Critical Essays* (New Jersey, 1963)

West, Rebecca, Preface to *Northanger Abbey* (London, 1932) pp. v-xi

Wharton, Edith, *The Writing of Fiction* (New York, 1925) pp. 128-30

Whately, Richard, *Quarterly Review* XXIV (1821) pp. 352-76

Wilks, Brian, *Jane Austen* (London, 1978)

Woolf, Virginia, Review of the *Life*, *TLS* (May 8th, 1913) pp. 189-90

——— 'Jane Austen at Sixty', *New Republic* 37 (1924) p. 261

Wright, Andrew, 'Jane Austen Adapted', *Nineteenth-Century Fiction* 30 (1975-6) pp. 421-53

——— *Jane Austen's Novels: A Study in Structure* (London, 1957)

Index

This is deliberately brief, and is divided as follows:

A. Jane Austen's works, main references
B. Selected general index

A.Works by Jane Austen

B. Selected general index

Amis, K., 94
Aristotle, 14
Auerbach, N., 8
Austen, Cassandra, 22, 24-5, 43, 49,
  55, 57, 60, 67, 69, 74, 93, 99,
  107-8
Austen, Charles, 27, 108-9, 123
Austen, Edward, 26, 53, 60, 107
Austen, Frank, 25, 27, 57-8, 108,
  119, 121
Austen, George, 107
Austen, George (father), 24-5, 57,
  104-5
Austen, Henry, 20-1, 27, 50, 59, 75,
  104, 107-8, 110, 117, 119
Austen, James, 106, 119
Austen, Mrs (mother), 105-6
Austen-Leigh, J.E., 22-4, 105-6, 109
Austen-Leigh, R., 24-7, 50, 117
Austen-Leigh, W., 24-7, 50, 117

Babb, H., 72-4
Bage, R., 86
Balzac, H. de, 30, 32
Bath, 25, 38, 44, 49, 50, 52, 57, 74,
  99, 100
Bayley, J., 3, 6
Bennett, Arnold, 41
Bentley, R., 12
Blackall, S., 25, 120
Blok, H. Abigail, 3
Boswell, J., 51
Bowen, E., 7
Bowen, M., 4
Bradbury, M., 94
Bradley, A.C., 32-3, 50
Brontë, Charlotte, 15-16, 31
Brydges, Sir E., 7, 23, 120
Burney, Fanny, 5, 35
Burrows, J.F., 128
Bush, D., 83-5

Butler, M., 7, 85-9, 101

Cecil, Lord David, 6-7, 51, 74, 95-6,
  110
Chapman, R.W., 9-10, 40, 49-52, 53,
  55-60, 124, 127
Chawton, 22-3, 26, 44, 50, 53, 58,
  74, 100, 112, 121-2
Chesterton, G.K., 33-4
Clarentine, 57
Clarke, J., 23, 59-60, 123
Congreve, William, 69
Cowper, William, 5
Crabbe, George, 5, 123
Craik, W.A., 70-2
Craven, C., 109
Crook, N., 117

Daiches, D., 65
Dallas, E.S., 18
Devlin, D.D., 81-3, 113
Doody, M.A., 124
Duckworth, A., 3
Duffy, J., 1

Eden, Emily, 6
Edgeworth, Maria, 14, 35, 87
Eliot, George, 18
Émile (Rousseau), 103

Farrer, R., 35-40, 127
Felix Holt, 18
Ferrier, S., 11-12
Feuillide, Comte de, 25
Feuillide, Eliza, 25, 49, 67, 107,
  119-20
Fielding, Henry, 15-16, 21, 66
Fitzgerald, Edward, 17
Forster, E.M., 40, 46, 51, 110
Frye, Northrop, 97